HITLER
GOD
& THE BIBLE

HITLER
GOD
& THE BIBLE

RAY
COMFORT

 WND Books

HITLER, GOD, AND THE BIBLE

WND Books
Washington, D.C.

Book Designed by Mark Karis

WND Books are distributed to the trade by:
Midpoint Trade Books
27 West 20th Street, Suite 1102
New York, NY 10011

WND Books are available at special discounts for bulk
purchases. WND Books, Inc., also publishes books in electronic
formats. For more information call (541) 474-1776
or visit www.wndbooks.com.

First Edition

ISBN 13 Digit: 978-1936488247

Library of Congress information available.

Printed in the United States of America.

· Dedication ·

To those who keep alive the memory of this
dark hour of human history

"And so I believe today that my conduct is in accordance with the will of the Almighty Creator. In standing guard against the Jew I am defending the handiwork of the Lord."

~ Adolf Hitler, Mein Kampf

· Table of Contents ·

· *Acknowledgments* ·

My sincere thanks to Manuel Brambila for his valuable research; to editor Lynn Copeland; and to WND, for having the vision to publish this series.

TIM LAHAYE

A S A YOUNG GI right after World War II, one of my most heartrending experiences was to visit Dachau near Munich, Germany, one of Hitler's terrible concentration camps. The stench of death still lingered over the place. It was indeed one of the most revolting experiences of the war. How could anyone be so inhumane as to round up millions of Jews, herd them like animals into a death camp, and incinerate them? Certainly it took a madman to give such orders. Adolf Hitler was just such a fiend. However, he was not always that evil. He gradually became that way as his fame and power grew. He went from being appointed chancellor of Germany to becoming the Führer or total dictator of the nation. Lord Acton is quoted as saying, "Power tends to corrupt and absolute power corrupts absolutely." Hitler is a classic example.

Ray Comfort is to be commended for this well-researched and well-written account of a notorious madman who inspired millions to share his insane hatred for those referred to as "God's chosen people," the Jews. Space does not permit that we list the thousands of brilliant Jews who used their intellectual gifts to advance humanity and humanitarian causes.

This book will both inform and inspire readers to do all they can to keep such a tragedy from being repeated against human beings in any country. All honest historians admit it was an indescribable horror that robbed millions of people of "life, liberty and the pursuit of happiness."

"And so, internally armed with faith in the goodness of God and the impenetrable stupidity of the electorate, the struggle for what is called 'the reconstruction of the REICH' can now begin."

~ Adolf Hitler

HUMAN BEINGS just can't seem to get along. Territory, natural resources, currency. We can summon disputes, verbal and physical lashings, from a kernel seed. Examine any segment of world history, and you'll find violence, rather than peaceful self-sufficiency, has been the dominating factor.

Violence, deception, and greed come naturally to humanity, in a world that continually beckons our depravity and darker instincts.

Throughout the years, I've looked closely at the wells from which we draw our wisdom, and I've found the topic of cultural icons and their influence on societies to be extremely compelling. Individuals in positions of power have the ability to shape and distort the public's opinion on a variety of life's most crucial matters, religion included. Even more disturbing is their ability to actually use religion as a tool to captivate, deceive, and manipulate.

Hitler, God, and the Bible is the first book in a series of concise and hopefully insightful exposés on the intersection of icons and faith.

When I began my research for this series, Hitler was a natural first subject. His rise to power and dominance over people and across boundaries was unprecedented. He used the modern state and media as weapons to manipulate and control the general populace. In an advanced, morally aware society, he was able to mobilize a movement that claimed the lives of millions of individuals. And it didn't take long to ignite. Just a handful of years after claiming power, he was defining a century by its blackest mark: genocide.

If you study the family trees of households today, particularly in Western society, you'll be hard-pressed to find a limb that wasn't altered or eliminated by Hitler's hand. My own family's is no exception.

In the late 1800s, my great-grandparents, who were Jewish, lived in Poland. It was still under Russian authority from when Catherine the Great invaded nearly a century earlier, and over the years anti-Semitism greatly increased, making it a very difficult place for my grandparents to live.

With the upper echelons of society calling for more severe measures every day, my great-grandparents were wise enough to see that the conditions for Jews wouldn't be improving. At the age of eight, my great grandparents hid their son in a clothes basket and smuggled him out of his homeland to the safety of Dover, England. Their decision to leave Poland proved to be a wise move. In the next decade Poland experienced mass emigration due to poverty, with approximately 4 million of the country's 22 million citizens emigrating to the United States prior to World War I.

In England, my family's name was changed to Cook, and Solomon grew up out of the tornado's eye. And it was there that he and my grandmother, Hilda, met and eloped when she was only seventeen years old, eventually settling in New Zealand where they had twelve children.

At age nineteen, my mother, Esther, fell in love with a handsome Gentile named Ray Comfort. Despite family opposition she married him, and was immediately ostracized by her parents for marrying out of the faith.

My dad fought against the Germans in the Second World War in the famous Seventh Armored Division, whose exploits were portrayed in the movie *The Desert Rats*. They were a group of British and Allied soldiers who were instrumental in the defeat of the Germans in North Africa. The Rats were especially noted for a hard-fought three-month campaign against the more experienced German Afrika Korps, led by General Erwin Rommel, who was known as "The Desert Fox."

With the Nazi Holocaust fresh on their minds, my parents decided to put "Methodist" rather than "Jew" on my birth certificate. At the age of nine I began praying each night, thanks to the encouragement of a loving Roman Catholic aunt. As I entered my teenage years, I also began reading the Bible. At that point in my life I could be thought of as a Jewish, praying, Bible-reading Methodist.

With my family's background, the subject of Hitler and his use of, and abuse of, the church is very personal to me. While whole libraries have been written documenting the history of Hitler's Third Reich, I hope what you read here casts fresh insight into the role of the church and its opponents during that critical point in history. In *Hitler, God, and the Bible*, we'll examine the life of Adolf Hitler and the propagandizing of the Christian church in Germany, with a special focus on the roles that God and the Bible played, either genuinely or exploitatively. While questions are difficult and answers hard to come by, we can all gain something from exploration and the desire to understand.

I certainly have, and it's my desire that you do, too.

· *Part 1* ·

DISCOVERING THE POLITICAL IDEOLOGUE

THE HISTORY OF ADOLF HITLER

"I must honestly confess that I would have preferred it if he had followed his original ambition and become an architect."

~ Paula Hitler, speaking of her brother Adolf

ORIGINS ARE CURIOUS THINGS, particularly when it comes to people. How someone was raised, and whether the person was taught love, discipline, and respect, can be markedly telling.

Born in Austria near the German border, Adolf

Hitler was raised by two highly contrasting characters who would play instrumental roles in his character development: on one side his father, Alois Hitler, and on the other his mother, Klara Hitler.

Alois, who came from a poor family and left home at age thirteen, was no doubt considered by some to be a success. At the age of eighteen, in 1855, he was employed at the Austrian Ministry of Finance and worked his way up to becoming a customs inspector. Alois was a prideful man who took great stock in his success. He changed his family name from Shicklgruber to Hitler, a swap he hoped would help his ladder-climbing potential. But as history duly notes, it was his son who benefited most.

Through Alois, the Hitler family was able to lead what would be considered a rather content life in the middle class. They had the means to be well fed and well cared for. Alois was respected in society and faithful to his position, but his duty as a civil servant often went to his head, resulting in rash changes of temper, a strict and unforgiving hand, and a pretentious disposition that was hardly enjoyable to share a roof with—characteristics Adolf would inherit and refine.

Alois came to marry three women in his life, fathering eight children. His third and final marriage, at age forty-eight, was to Klara Pölzl, his second cousin twenty-three years his junior, who became pregnant while Alois' second wife was freshly in the ground. Klara's first three children all passed away before the age of three, one at childbirth and the other two just a few months later to diphtheria. But on April 20, 1889—Easter Saturday, no less—she gave birth to a child who would live: Adolf Hitler. Perhaps fearful of losing him too, Klara coddled Adolf, even after the birth of another son and daughter. Edmund would die just shy of age six of measles, and only Paula, seven years younger than Adolf, would survive into adulthood.

In contrast with Alois, Klara was a gentle, quiet spirit. She was obedient in all, burying the sorrows of an angry, ill-tempered husband and a stolen youth by keeping close watch of their children, including the two born by Alois' previous wife. But it was Klara's own children she doted on most and protected from the hands of quick-fisted Alois. While Adolf was prone to earn the chastisement of his father thanks to childish prodding and misbehavior, he knew his mother to be a safe haven, and for that he loved her. Throughout life into adulthood, his opinions of women were small and condescending. His mother was one of perhaps only two females he ever sincerely loved and valued.

Paula, Adolf's younger sister, noted their

mother to be "a very soft and tender person, the compensatory element between the almost too harsh father and the very lively children who perhaps were somewhat difficult to train. If there were ever quarrel or difference of opinion between my parents," she noted, "it was always on account of the children. It was especially my brother Adolf who challenged my father to extreme harshness and who got his sound thrashing every day...How often on the other hand did my mother caress him and try to obtain with her kindness, where the father could not succeed with harshness!"[1]

AN EDUCATION

As a young child, Adolf was at first highly adaptable and eager for the company of others. By the time he was only nine years old, his family had uprooted multiple times, and he was enrolled in his third elementary school. He quickly befriended his classmates, and they spent many hours of the day caught up in war games. But with the completion of elementary school came the end of such joyful pursuits. Adolf's father enrolled him in a technical school that leaned heavily on scientific subjects, insistent that his son follow in his footsteps and begin a career in the civil service.

Alois's expectations for his son grew to be the largest point of contention in their relationship and one about which they battled frequently. While Alois had worked hard to rise above his prior station, Adolf showed none of the same ambition or work ethic. Instead, Adolf had a love for painting, and his self-proclaimed goal in life was to become a grand artist. Adolf didn't want his father, or anyone else for that matter, directing his actions. While Adolf was still young, his behavior even among his friends was reflective of the man he would become. When he didn't get his way—or if others proposed that they had better solutions—Adolf would immaturely shout over his own ignorance and feel a great deal of self-pity. There was never any sign of remorse. He was not one to admit fault or the need for self-improvement. Growing stubborn and domineering, Adolf was becoming well liked by few.

As his stalemate with his father continued, Adolf decided to sabotage his studies. Thinking that failing to do well in the technical school would convince his father to let him follow his dream of painting, Adolf applied himself only in subjects that he thought an artist would need. The rest he ignored.

When Adolf was just thirteen, this stalemate came to a sudden end: his father died of heart failure in 1903. The arguments over his profession were buried along with him. His mother, submissive as always, did little to push him in any direction. When he supposedly developed a lung illness, Adolf convinced his mother to let him leave school. For a time, Adolf indulged. He was taken care of at home, and he whittled away his hours by dreaming, drawing, and writing. Four short years after his father's death, he would be orphaned at age eighteen: he would lose his beloved mother to breast cancer.

It's easy to see that accountability was absent in Adolf's youth. His father's swift hand and sharp tongue did nothing but stir in him a desire to rebel and a strong distaste for authority, while his mother's pampering nature made her easy to manipulate and exploit. He never felt responsible, only entitled—a theme that would have devastating repercussions in the Nazi regime.

But in the meantime, politics weren't Adolf's agenda. His only ambition was to attend the Academy of Fine Arts in Vienna. Ambition, however, might be the wrong word as it implies some degree of drive and determination. Adolf simply believed he would be accepted and that he would go on to excel. No part of him could fathom that the opposite could occur. But in October 1907, shortly before his mother died, Adolf went to Vienna to take the entrance exam. His plan did not go accordingly, and his pride was dealt a most unexpected blow: he was rejected. With his mother's health deteriorating, he returned home, too ashamed to share the news, and dutifully stayed by his mother's side until she passed away a few days before Christmas. Adolf, who had formed such a strong attachment to his mother, was devastated by her death. After she was gone, he would return to Vienna.

Having the privilege of perspective, one can look at Adolf in his youth and know what he became. There was a vanity, even in his young self, that was uncompromising and unrealistic. He was domineering in all of his relationships, a trait he no doubt learned from his father, and because of this heavy-handed approach in all of his dealings, he did not experience closeness with others—the only exception, perhaps, being his mother.

THE VIENNA YEARS

Hitler returned to Vienna in February 1908, a city he would come to loathe and yet would remain in for the next five years. In his own words in *Mein Kampf*, Hitler wrote, "I am thankful for that period of my life, because it hardened me and enabled me to be as tough as I now am. And I am even more thankful because I appreciate the fact that I was thus saved from the emptiness of a life of ease and that a mother's darling was taken from tender arms and handed over to Adversity as to a new mother. Though I then rebelled against it as too hard a fate, I am grateful that I was thrown into a world of misery and poverty and thus came to know the people for whom I was afterwards to fight."[2]

In typical fashion, Hitler outdid himself. He bent truths and promulgated falsehoods to create the character of Hitler that people could associate with, sympathize with, and ultimately revere. Hitler understood well how to manipulate people, and he played on their malleable hearts and minds with exaggerations.

While in *Mein Kampf* he would claim that his mother's death left him in a grief-stricken state with barely a penny to live on, the tale is only partially true. Though Hitler's heart was no doubt wrecked by the loss of his mother, it was his ego that was in disrepair, not his bank account. He had his orphan's pension, money from his mother, and a generous loan for school from an aunt unaware of his rejection from the Academy of Fine Arts. He could not live extravagantly, but he could certainly live. And if he had the mind for employment and success, or even survival, he would have done fine by any standards.

But Hitler was disillusioned. He couldn't believe that his future as a grand artist was not as apparent to others as it was to himself. Yet instead of creating a plan, improving, or moving forward, Hitler lied, wallowed, and spent what money he had. Unlike Alois, Hitler was not born with nothing. He was not taught to work hard and rise above. Though only middle class, he fostered a strong feeling of privilege that left no room for dirt under his fingers or the word "no."

When he attempted to apply to the Academy of Fine Arts again in October 1908, they didn't even leave room for rejection; he was simply told he couldn't take the exam. Again, rather than find his bootstraps, he clung to a wounded ego and indulged in his dreams of being an artist, rather than having the ambition of one. And though he displayed a talent for drawing and was advised to apply to the School of Architecture, he lacked the necessary qualifications. He later admitted regret that the studies he had neglected out of spite for his father prevented him from completing his school diploma, a poor decision that closed another door of opportunity to him.

In the fall of 1909, Hitler experienced the poverty he claimed to have fallen into after his mother's death. Having completely exhausted his savings, he was forced to leave his accommodations and slept outdoors. When the weather became too bitter, he found barely tolerable accommodations that would at least provide a roof over his head. By Christmas, he had nothing left and found lodging at the homeless shelter. It was by far his lowest point.

In 1910, Hitler left the homeless shelter after receiving a small allowance from his Aunt Johanna and moved to a Men's Home for the poor in the north of the city. He made a meager living selling original postcard paintings at pubs, and to frame-makers and upholsterers who used cheap illustrations. Reinhold Hanisch, who helped Hitler peddle the postcards and then split the income, complained of Hitler's laziness and unwillingness to produce his art at a reasonable speed, a sentiment that would have come as no surprise to Hitler's father.

But it was also here, at the Men's Home, that the first signs of Hitler's political life began emerging. Political debates among regulars were frequent, and Hitler, now age twenty-one, was one of the most heated participants. Certain residents took issue with his violent attacks on the Social Democrats, and all were often forced to listen to his wild lectures on the German Radical Party; Karl Leuger, the anti-Semitic mayor of Vienna; and the wonders of Richard Wagner's music, among other things.

After such an existence—rejection, poverty, and homelessness—it's no surprise that Hitler hated Vienna. But despite how much Hitler desired to move past that time, the Vienna years proved to be a significant marker in his life for two primary reasons.

For starters, Hitler's time there fostered his irrational view of success. In Vienna, he relied heavily on appearances over realities. If he could have people believe he was living in the city as a successful artist, to him that was just as important as actually being one. When it came down to it, it was a simple need to be respected. Hitler wanted and needed to be thought well of, and he would do anything to protect and promote his image—for example, he continued telling people he was a student at the Academy of Fine Arts rather than admit failure and begin looking for opportunities elsewhere. To him, it was paramount to preserve his self-image and the "success" of his dream even at the expense of his physical comfort. In Vienna, defending this lie led to his poverty and homelessness.

Unfortunately, Hitler didn't learn from his mistakes. As the years progressed, he would only continue to live in a state of altered reality. Later in life, when his actions had massive reverberations that would impact not only all of Germany, but the majority of continental Europe, he would continue to protect and preserve his "truths" even to the detriment of many. Such egotism was one of his largest downfalls as a leader, and an Achilles heel that would ultimately bring him and his monstrous Nazi regime down.

Secondly, the Vienna years were important as they fostered some of Hitler's most integral ideologies, effectively shaping his prejudices—particularly against the Jews—as well as his irrational fears. At the time of Hitler's stay, Vienna was strained at all levels—socially, culturally, and politically. Hitler's favorite composer, Richard Wagner, was at his peak, and his music's anti-Semitism seeped into Hitler's bones and formed its stronghold. The city that beat Hitler down also built up those he despised, making the years fertile breeding ground for hatred. In *Mein Kampf*, Hitler wrote:

> It was during this period that my eyes were opened to two perils, the names of which I scarcely knew hitherto and had no notion whatsoever of their terrible significance for the existence of the German people. These two perils were Marxism and Judaism.

For many people the name of Vienna signifies innocent jollity, a festive place for happy mortals. For me, alas, it is a living memory of the saddest period in my life. Even to-day the mention of that city arouses only gloomy thoughts in my mind. Five years of poverty in that Phaecian town. Five years in which, first as a casual labourer and then as a painter of little trifles, I had to earn my daily bread. And a meager morsel indeed it was, not even sufficient to still the hunger which I constantly felt. That hunger was the faithful guardian which never left me but took part in everything I did. Every book that I bought meant renewed hunger, and every visit I paid to the opera meant the intrusion of that inalienable companion during the following days. I was always struggling with my unsympathic friend. And yet during that time I learned more than I had ever learned before. Outside my architectural studies and rare visits to the opera, for which I had to deny myself food, I had no other pleasure in life except my books.

I read a great deal then, and I pondered deeply over what I read. All the free time after work was devoted exclusively to study. Thus within a few years I was able to acquire a stock of knowledge which I find useful even to-day.

But more than that. During those years a view of life and a definite outlook on the world took shape in my mind. These became the granite basis of my conduct at that time.*3*

In Vienna, an irreversible course of hatred was set. What he lacked was a vehicle to use it. His coming years in Munich would be pivotal.

MUNICH

Hitler's escape from Austria to Germany came on his twenty-fourth birthday, and none too soon. His funds were sharply depleted and he could finally claim his share of his father's inheritance. With money in tow, he was able to pack his bags for Munich, the capital of the German state of Bavaria. Hitler's hatred for Vienna thrived and he found the German Empire to be his true calling where he could pursue a career as an architect—another dream that would end in failure. While it's true that Hitler believed the Austro-Hungarian Empire was living on borrowed time and full of corrupt ideology, another factor certainly played into his departure: Hitler had been skirting the Austrian military for three years, stubbornly refusing to serve his required time in the army. They were on to him, however, and would pursue him as soon as he left the country. A stroke of luck (an officer sympathetic to Hitler's haggard appearance and ill health) was the only thing that kept him out of an Austrian prison. His political career was affected by this a decade or so later, as he struggled to hide the fact that he had avoided military service at all costs.

Hitler lived in Munich for fifteen months before the start of World War I, a time which he proclaimed "by far the happiest and most contented" in his life. In contrast to the melting pot of Vienna, Munich was a German city. Its pure blood had not been tainted and corrupted by various undesirable races. And yet, Hitler's days there were really no different from his time in Vienna. He was all talk; as much as he described himself as an "architectural painter," his existence was similar to his days in the Men's Home: selling about one postcard every three days, reading books, and getting into political arguments with whoever would participate. For more than a year he was in many ways continuing a state of vegetation. It would take something massive to jolt him out of his lethargy. Something that would ignite his passions and his actions.

And indeed a stroke of luck occurred. In June 1914, the Austrian Archduke Franz Ferdinand and his wife were assassinated in Sarajevo. World War I broke out and the German Empire went to the aid of Austria-Hungary. The beer halls and public arenas thrived with national pride and political prattle. Adolf Hitler finally had a cause, not to mention a sense of belonging, for the first time in his life.

HITLER ENTERS
THE POLITICAL
REALM

"I sank down upon my knees and thanked Heaven
out of the fullness of my heart for the favour of
having been permitted to live in such a time."

~ *Adolf Hitler, Mein Kampf*

OR MOST PEOPLE, war represents the culmination of their fears. It is party to death, dread, and unnameable, impending difficulties. Even in the face of honor and principle, a declaration of war is rarely a cause for joy. But for Adolf Hitler, World War I was exactly what he had been waiting for.

Prior to the war, Hitler was, by all accounts, a nobody. He had latched onto his dreams of notoriety and found them to be hollow and unattainable. Despite his love for art, his actions did not indicate that he was a man with any capacity for dedication. Perhaps his only release and sense of belonging were found in the cafes and beer halls where he could prattle on with his well-known passion and not be required to back up his claims with any substantial actions.

World War I represented the moment in history where Hitler first felt anything cementing him in a future. There was belonging. The diatribes that had spilled so frequently off his tongue were now flowing from the mouths of his countrymen.

ENLISTING

Despite his many years evading military service in the Austria he detested, the declaration of war created in Hitler a sense of national pride—only it wasn't in his own birthplace. Germany, though not his homeland, had become his heartland, and he felt the surge to serve just as every other able-bodied man did who stood up quickly and enthusiastically to enlist. By error on account of the multitudes of volunteers, he became an Austrian in the Bavarian army.

Contrasting the fervent call to arms, war was a startling and heavy blow of reality. In less than a week of fighting, Hitler's regiment lost 70 percent of its men. Those who survived were constant spectators to injury and death. While many of the men clung together in this trying time of loss and bloodshed, an already distant, emotionally remote Hitler was taught to care even less. He was constantly on the fringes, never joining in the camaraderie that provided one of the few respites to war's terrors.

Yet despite his distance, Hitler's time in the service was critical to his formation as a political and social leader. Without World War I, there wouldn't have been a Führer or Nazi Germany. His love for the state was brought to an entirely new level, and unlike his previous years of being full of words and promises and empty of action, Hitler was a committed soldier. He did not shirk from duty; he did not shy from danger. Unlike anything prior, he was compelled to commitment. As a dispatch runner, Corporal Hitler eagerly volunteered for dangerous assignments and was noted for his courage. He received five medals, including the Iron Cross Second Class and the Iron Cross First Class, both of which he wore until he died. By the end of the war, he found himself among the injured, confined to a hospital due to temporary blindness following a British mustard gas attack.

During his time in the infantry, Hitler displayed a tremendous vigor evident through both his actions and his words. He loudly detested any mention of defeat, and was disgusted by the growing attitude of disdain and desertion found among his compatriots at the front. In *Hitler: A Biography*, Ian Kershaw speculates that Hitler's time on leave in Berlin interacting with the civilian population, as well as his time in the hospital, probably played a large part in his severe ideological developments: he was appalled by the growing attitude of revolution against the German monarchy, portrayed in such events as a munitions strike in favor of an early peace without annexations.[1]

Simply put, while other soldiers were loyal to one another, Hitler was loyal to the state. To him, that was the relationship to fight to preserve. A soldier could die, but the state, above all, must live.

END OF WORLD WAR I

By the end of 1918, the war was coming to a close. Turkey made peace, followed by Austria. On November 9, Kaiser Wilhelm II abdicated and on November 11, Germany signed an armistice with the

Allies, officially ending World War I. When the message finally reached Hitler in the hospital regarding Germany's defeat and the collapse of the monarchy in Berlin, he fell into a deep and utter despair. Everything he had joined himself to and fought so hard for had fallen apart.

The Second Reich came to an end and a troubled democracy took its place. Defeat in war brought the severe unrest at home to a head. Growing from 1915 onward, military failure and desertion by soldiers proved to a population that the once spirited and united Germany was plunging quickly and no longer worth fighting for. Individuals picked the scapegoat of their choice—among them war profiteering, bureaucratic intrusion in everyday life, and one that would become all too familiar: Jews.

As in times before and in many times to come, Hitler used the situation to further embed his preexisting beliefs. To him it wasn't possible that the German population clamored for uprisings because of a lack of military success; indeed to him it was the opposite. The unrest at home was the reason the military failed. The complete lack of appreciation and reverence for Germany appalled him, emboldening his long-held views on the effects of Jews, Social Democrats, and Marxism. To Hitler, they were the expendable ones and the state their victim. They were the guilty party responsible for undermining the war effort, leading to Germany's failure.

Yet Germany's defeat in World War I was a substantial building block in the Third Reich. In order for a drastic new government, such as the Nazi regime, to become politically viable, the citizens would have to feel a need for national change. For the majority of Germans, the Versailles Treaty and its call for disarmament was humiliating. Signed in 1919, the Treaty conceded German territories to Belgium, Czechoslovakia, Poland, and France. It required demilitarization and occupation of the Rhineland, as well as dismantling of the air force and a limit of 100,000 men in the army. Germany was likewise required to accept the War Guilt Clause, which stated Germany started World War I and was thus responsible for its cost. The required reparation payments, then equivalent to $31.4 billion U.S., were insurmountable.

A culture and country deeply dependent on ego found itself sprawled, the defeated beggar, on the world's stage. The coming leaders' lack of success in the following decades would only increase public desire for political change.

While Hitler had demonstrated little to no interest in leadership thus far, his propensity for politics was unparalleled. With no family or friends to speak of, the state was the only important thing in his life.

UNREST IN THE HOMELAND

When Hitler was discharged from the hospital in November 1918, he had been in the army for four years. He was twenty-nine years old, burdened by a deep pain and anger on behalf of his abandoned Germany, and had no prospects of where to go. While most soldiers were disbanded or disinterested in further national service, Hitler found nothing but a need to serve. Without the army, where would he go?

Hitler remained in the military and was stationed in Munich, which he found in a state of upheaval. Politically driven civil conflict erupted, dissolving the imperial regime. Kurt Eisner, of the Independent Social Democratic Party, played a pivotal role in overthrowing the monarchy of Bavaria, declaring it a Socialist Republic. Eisner was ultimately assassinated and a whirlwind of governments, led by Social Democrats and Communists, filtered through. The revolution wouldn't end until the formation of the Weimar Republic in 1919. And while Hitler largely kept his head down as the government flipped and flopped, the revolution was a public demonstration of national dissatisfaction and it cemented for Hitler, as it did for many others, the need for a clear and effective revival. Oddly it was the Weimar Republic, which Hitler would inevitably overtake nearly two decades later, which would provide Hitler with ample footing for leadership growth.

In May 1919, after the army crushed a Communist takeover, Hitler helped identify those involved in the uprising. He was then chosen to be a part of a team of officers to undergo educational courses on political and ideological thinking. He lapped it up, submerging himself in his education and, afterward, in disseminating his political and social beliefs to troops.

The truth was that even though the revolution was over, the fledgling German democratic republic was in dire trouble and entirely vulnerable. They needed to reign in stability. Until they could do that, attacks both political and physical would come from all sides. The extreme right (whom Hitler would soon rally) missed the existence of a monarchy, and the extreme left (who originated the attempted Communist takeover) had no use for a republic. But there was a third and equally dangerous threat that came from below where the true reins of power had always been held in Germany: by the German army.

The democratic republic was aware that winning people's minds was equivalent to winning the fight. Propaganda was an essential component, and the government needed able voices to disseminate their message. Hitler gained quick notoriety as an articulate and passionate speaker, and the authorities proposed that he join a local army organization that was convincing returning soldiers not to join the Communists or Pacifists. The job gave him a lot of practice speaking persuasively, and he greatly sharpened his oratory skills during this time.

It's safe to say that from 1919 onward, a new face of Hitler emerged. In the years prior he had been a footnote, occasionally a figure of mockery. Certainly no one would have pegged him as the great, coming Führer. There had yet to be seen any of the extraordinary charisma and appeal that would later lure and convince the masses. He had not been distinctive or memorable in the slightest. But stepping into the spotlight with his repertoire of propaganda, adoration followed. People flocked to him. They listened to him. Through his oratory fireworks, he became known as an individual who could provide promising answers for the future.

To understand Hitler's success, it is essential to understand the needs of the people who lived in his time. Germany was in ruins. Society was traumatized at all levels. Following World War I, there was a sense of heavy embarrassment, failure, and deep-seated need. People wanted a savior. So when Hitler began talking, they slowly sat up to listen.

THE GERMAN WORKERS' PARTY

As a corporal in the German army, Hitler was tasked with sniffing out and then undermining the efforts of opposing parties who could pose potential threats. He would venture into their party meetings as a spy and serve as the standard fly on the wall, reporting what he'd heard. In September 1919, he was ordered to spy on the German Workers' Party (abbreviated DAP), one of the countless political parties that seemed likely to instigate civil uprisings. But this meeting went differently than planned. Hitler could not hold his tongue when he disagreed with a guest about the purity of the German race. Anton Drexler, the party's founder, was so impressed with Hitler and his oratory skills that he asked him to join the organization. Feeling compelled by the party's nationalist ideas and his own ability to communicate that message, Hitler joined the party, writing that the organization offered "a chance for real personal activity on the part of the individual." Even more appealing, it was small enough to be molded to his liking: "as the movement was still small, one could all the easier give it the required shape. Here it was still possible to determine the character of the movement, the aims to be achieved and the road to be taken, which would have been impossible in the case of the big parties already existing."[2] In 1920 to broaden the organization's appeal, Hitler changed its name to the National Socialist German Workers' Party (abbreviated NSDAP)—more commonly referred to as the Nazi Party.

When Hitler was discharged from the army of the Weimar Republic on March 31, 1920, he decided to devote his time fully to the NSDAP and the duties of promotion and propaganda. It was in this capacity that he found and honed his gift: speaking. Thanks to his command of word and stage, he soon found himself able to attract large crowds and big donations. "Without his self-discovery that he could 'speak,'" wrote biographer Ian Kershaw, "he would not have been able to contemplate the possibility of making a living from politics. But without the extraordinary political climate of post-war Germany, and, quite especially, the unique conditions in Bavaria, Hitler would have found himself in any case without an audience, his 'talent' pointless and unrecognized, his tirades of hate without echo, the backing from those close to the avenues of power, on whom he depended, unforthcoming."[3]

But as history would have it, the world of politics opened up to Hitler, and he finally gained the assurance that he would never live as a starving artist again.

BECOMING A FIGUREHEAD

It didn't take long to start building the legend of Hitler. Within four years of joining the party, he was a local figurehead, amassing supporters and devotees.

Hitler's ideology was in the beginning what it would be in the end, though dispelled in more watered-down, socially appealing rhetoric. Like all the warring parties clamoring for leadership, the NSDAP promised a restored Germany. Hitler took podium after podium, claiming that his party was for the people and that his methods were for a better way of life, one that existed before World War I and the hated Versailles Treaty. But in politics as in the army, his concern wasn't for the individual, but for the state the individual served. Few were wise to the truth and even fewer wanted to be.

The beginning of the Nazi Party was fueled by emotion. If you sat through one of Hitler's speeches, you would probably have left inspired, full of anger for the administration, and resolve to change the circumstances of your life and your country. But if you really thought about it, truly and deeply thought about it, you would have found little sustenance in the words and promises that came flowing out of his mouth. He prodded people's heart strings, but he didn't give practical ways to heal the hurts.

Down with the Republic! Up with the Nazis! came the shouts.

But what would a Nazi regime mean? Everyone was in too much of a hurry to ask.

In 1920, a solid foundation for the party was forming. The eventual pillars of the Third Reich (Heinrich Himmler, Hermann Goering, and Rudolf Hess) joined the NSDAP, and Hitler designed an official symbol to represent the party: he chose the swastika, an ancient symbol used by many cultures throughout history, and placed it in bold white, red, and black. While the symbol was not one he invented, he infused it with his own ideology: "The red expressed the social thought underlying the movement. White the national thought. And the swastika signified the mission allotted to us—the struggle for the victory of Aryan mankind and at the same time the triumph of the ideal of creative work which is in itself and always will be anti-Semitic."[4]

While Hitler's ideas were not groundbreaking, how he communicated with the people was. He spoke passionately and effectively and attracted attention. He was not afraid of confrontation and even invited it, and formed a private group to squelch any disruptions at his party's meetings as well as break up the opposition parties' meetings. This group, distinguished by their brown shirts, was known as the Sturmabteilung (SA, "Storm Troopers"), or "Brownshirts."

By 1921, Hitler was the face of the movement—though still not the Chairman. Drexler knew the people flocked to Hitler, but Hitler was too aware of his weaknesses when it came to organizing and logistically propelling the engine forward. He could mobilize the masses, propaganda was his lifeblood, but he shied away from the responsibility of having to manage everything. It could be argued that, at the time, Hitler didn't see himself as the future leader who would save the nation. While he maintained his ego and all-or-nothing attitude in his interactions, he told a newspaper that he was not "the architect who clearly pictured in his own eyes the plan and design of the new building and with calm sureness and creativity was able to lay one stone on the other. He needed the greater one behind him, on whose command he could lean."[5]

The peculiar thing was, the Nazi Party was not founded as a group that clung with undue importance to leadership. As Kershaw has pointed out, "The word 'leader' ('Führer') had no special meaning attached to it. Every political party or organization had a leader—or more than one. The NSDAP was no different. Drexler was referred to as the party's 'Führer,' as was Hitler; or sometimes both in practically the same breath. Once Hitler had taken over the party leadership in July 1921, the term 'our leader' ('unser Führer') became gradually more common. But its meaning was still interchangeable with the purely functional 'chairman of the NSDAP.'"[6]

More than being about a leader, the NSDAP was about a takeover. The current administration had to go whatever the costs. And while the NSDAP was certainly gaining popularity, they were far from the majority. To many they were still a risky fringe group who needed to prove themselves. They had to be more than beer-hall talkers who shouted their ambitions like college boys. They had to have something they clearly lacked: an organized plan to usurp and implement.

The failure of the NSDAP as an organized and intentional party became widely apparent in the fall of 1922 when whispers ran through the streets that Hitler was planning a coup. By the New Year, the idea of a takeover was on the lips of nearly all citizens. Unrest was at an all-time high. The combination of the fledgling government, war debt, and reparations owed to Allied nations left Germany's economy in ruins. Before reparations, it took four German marks to buy one American dollar. By November 1923, it was four trillion marks to one U.S. dollar. The people saw the new government as traitorous, fraudulent, and ineffective. Hitler knew the government was vulnerable.

The power vacuum made conditions perfectly ripe for Hitler and the Nazi Party to make their move. By this time Hitler had practically gained total control of the Party, and despite its relatively small size and significance, on November 8, 1923, Hitler's Brownshirts attempted to overthrow the local Bavarian government in Munich. Hitler's idea of kidnapping the Bavarian officials as they were gathered at a local beer hall was poorly planned and even more poorly executed. What is known as the "Beer Hall Putsch" (or military coup d'etat) ended in failure. It was a passionate, but ill-drafted attempt to take power.

The Munich police defeated them. Hitler was arrested and charged with treason. Even though the constitution at the time called for lifelong imprisonment for revolutionaries, he successfully used his trial to promote his ideas and himself, swaying the judges to overlook his Austrian citizenship and admire his German patriotism. Hitler was sentenced to a mere five years in prison. Clearly even though he was still learning, there was something to Hitler that made even his enemies give way.

· *3* ·

THE RISE OF
NAZI GERMANY

"After fifteen years of work I have achieved,
as a common German soldier and merely with
my fanatical will-power, the unity of the German
nation, and have freed it from the death sentence
of Versailles."

~ Adolf Hitler, proclamation to the troops,
Dec. 21, 1941

HITLER WAS RIGHT about one thing: Germany's leadership was full of weakness. Punished with a mere slap on the wrist of five years in prison, he would ultimately serve less than a year in conditions that seemed more fit for a restoring hideaway than prison confinement.

While the Beer Hall Putsch had not been a success, the trial afterward was. Hitler was quoted widely throughout the media, expanding his audience and followers to all corners of Germany. Speaking in his own defense, Hitler was able to use the courtroom as a venue to express his ideas at length, ideas that he continued to formulate and pen while he was behind bars. While perhaps the execution of the Putsch had been poor, the repercussions set the stage for Hitler to mature in his visions and as a leader.

On April 1, 1924, Hitler was sent to Landsberg Prison to serve his sentence. But Landsberg was hardly punishment. To the contrary, it was a time of rebuilding that allowed Hitler to cement his ideologies. Confined to a private cell that was spacious and comfortable, he received flowers, gifts, and letters in multitudes. He was given the privilege of a secretary and was occasionally—when no one was watching—addressed by his guards with a "Heil Hitler." It was the life of a hero, not a traitor.

What Landsberg provided more than anything, though, was clarity, both for Hitler and for the German people. With Hitler behind bars, the movement on the right experienced a vacuum in leadership. The faction splintered, not able to find a voice or a name to rally behind. In contrast, stepping away from the limelight and the talking points, Hitler was able to finally put a finger on what he had been denying and perhaps hadn't even fully realized before—there was no reason to keep looking for a leader; he was Germany's deliverance.

At the time of Hitler's confinement, Rudolf Hess was also serving time for his role in the Beer Hall Putsch. At Landsberg, the two had plenty of time to philosophize ideas about Germany's future. Hitler dictated his thoughts and philosophy, and Hess wrote them down in what became the book *Mein Kampf* ("My Struggle"). Hitler believed Germany had to expand east, eliminate the Jews (whom he blamed for Germany's political and economical problems), and turn Slavs into slaves. He said that he had to take control of Germany legally and not by force. In *Mein Kampf*, Hitler clearly laid out his idea of a New Order in full throughout the manuscript, giving everyone fair warning of what he would do if he came to power. Needless to say, it's to the world's great detriment that no one listened.

A MORE INTENTIONAL LEADER

Hitler was released from prison on December 20, 1924—three years and 333 days short of his already lenient sentence. He was equipped with more thoroughly developed philosophies and was determined not to rehash the mistakes that had been made with rushed ignorance at the Beer Hall Putsch. To gain power, Hitler decided he would not topple the government by a rebellion, but would be elected: "Instead of working to achieve power by an armed coup," he said, "we shall have to hold our noses and enter the Reichstag against the Catholic and Marxist deputies. If outvoting them takes longer than outshooting them, at least the results will be guaranteed by their own Constitution! Any lawful process is slow. But sooner or later we shall have a majority—and after that Germany."[1]

Upon his release from prison, Hitler began his integration back into the Party and into the public eye. The dilapidation of the Nazi Party in Hitler's absence demanded immediate and stringent rebuilding. As a first order of business, a mere two weeks after being released from prison, Hitler found himself in the company of the Prime Minister of Bavaria.

Over the course of three meetings, the Prime Minister would allow the Nazi Party to regroup if they agreed to respect the authority of the State and played by its rules, among other stipulations. Hitler agreed, but at the first public rally since the Beer Hall

Putsch, Hitler's diatribe—not surprisingly—slipped into the same footholds it had been accustomed to, and the Bavarian government banned Hitler from public speaking for two years. But that was not a deterrent for the revitalized leader. Hitler threw himself into an overhaul of the Nazi government with two goals: undermine and overtake the current leadership, and have a government in the wings that could step in immediately.

With the NSDAP in shambles, Hitler knew he had intensive work ahead that would require significant time and a capable, devoted team. He was perceptive enough to be openhanded to those who courted control and were influential in the community. Rather than suspect them and cast them aside, he gave them positions of leadership. Gregor Strasser became the propaganda leader, Franz Pfeffer head of the SA, and the initially skeptical Joseph Goebbels became Hitler's second in command. "I believe he has taken me to his heart like no one else," Goebbels wrote. "Adolf Hitler, I love you because you are both great and simple at the same time. What one calls a genius."[2]

By 1926, the Nazi Party had still not regained the members it boasted prior to the Putsch. But this was of little concern to Hitler or ranking party members. They were more organized and clear in communication than ever before. They were developing deep roots that could harness power and multitudes effectively when the time came. No longer rushing or preoccupied with immediacy, Hitler and his comrades were being something they hadn't been before: intentional.

To this end they instituted a number of new and improved agendas. Two of the most important were the formation of the Hitler Youth, which would rear young boys in the Nazi agenda, and the transformation of the SA—Hitler's monitoring troop—into a crew that would be more authoritative and appealing to the masses. Within the SA, Hitler formed the SS (Schutzstaffel, "Protection Squad") whose members would serve as Hitler's personal bodyguards.

But the most important intention was a new perception of Hitler. While previously he had been the grandstanding, approachable mouthpiece for the party's message, he was now building a contrived reverence for himself. Access to Hitler was rare. He deliberately played up a sense of mystery and awe surrounding his character. He would deliberately arrive late to build anticipation, was theatrical in presentation—captivating—and then would exit at the crescendo, leaving everyone wanting more.

When individuals were given an opportunity to meet him, he played up his character, leaving a remarkable impression. And all of this was part of a large orchestration to make people believe that they needed and wanted him.

What he began building from the day he left prison was the cult of Hitler. In a speech on February 27, 1925, he said his great responsibility was "bringing together again those who are going different ways."[3] By driving the necessity of a great leader to harness and unify, Hitler positioned himself as the political and social messiah Germany had been waiting for.

As the underpinnings of the Nazi Party were being driven into place, it was crucial for Hitler to expand his reach. Not only was it important in fostering the leadership cult and bringing votes to his side when the time came, but it was also essential for the Party's stability. Like any other organization, it ran off donations, and the Nazis knew they needed to delve into the bureaucrats' pockets to line their own.

While the trial and his imprisonment expanded Hitler's audience, it was necessary to reach those who might not as quickly adopt his loose-lipped slurs against the Jews. Particularly concerning the north of Germany, he had to identify and address their social concerns while providing them with a political program that would be resolute. Knowing their likes and dislikes, Hitler preached intolerance, violence, and superiority. They loved him for it.

And while his followers steadily grew, the people failed to see that there were no concrete policies behind Hitler's overreaching schemes. Certainly the Nazi Party had improved since the Beer Hall Putsch. They were far more organized and were preaching about what they wanted as much as what they didn't. But what was missing was the detail. As Kershaw points out, "Political struggle, eventual attainment of power, destruction of the enemy, and build-up of the nation's might were stepping-stones to the goal,"[4] but little energy was put into fleshing out those concepts more intricately. The Nazi Party was a propaganda rat race with the ultimate focus on hoodwinking the people. Their goal was to prove themselves the most viable and attractive option as future leader. But if they succeeded, what would be implemented?

NEEDING THE NAZIS

The years 1925–1928 certainly provided strides in Hitler's notoriety, but his rule was not absolute. In order for Hitler to succeed and implement his dictator-run government, the people would need a reason to rally behind him, and that reason would have to be extreme discontent. Since Hitler's release from prison, a new and unexpected opposition emerged: Germany was improving. In 1925, Paul von Hindenburg was elected as the second president of Germany after President Friedrich Ebert's death. The Weimar Republic adopted a unique form of presidential government, enacting the 25/48/53 formula, which gave key roles to the president, the chancellor (who served as the head of state, similar to the role of prime minister), and the Reichstag (the parliament). The 25/48/53 formula referred to the articles in the constitution that would provide checks and balances. Article 25 gave the president the ability to dissolve the Reichstag. Article 48 gave the President the ability to sign laws into passage without the Reichstag's vote; however, if the majority of the Reichstag voted against the measure within sixty days, it would be considered null and void. Article 53 gave the president the ability to name the chancellor. Under this formula, the economy was healing and industry was rebuilding. Currency stabilized. As a result, the constituency of the disgruntled dwindled and with it the numbers in the Nazi Party. Hitler knew the simple truth: he had to keep casting his nets and bide his time until unhappiness prevailed again.

By late 1928, cracks were again showing in the economy. Unemployment reached three million in January 1929, and there was a growing crisis in agriculture. As life in Germany worsened, the Nazi Party—as expected—gained more favorable support. Within the first few months of the year, Hitler added fuel to the fire, writing articles for the Party press and giving sixteen speeches. He constantly emphasized that change was necessary, penning phrases such as, "The entire system must be altered. Therefore, the great task is to restore to people their belief in leadership."[5]

By mid-1929, the Party's numbers were up to 130,000, and on October 29, 1929, Hitler received the gift he had been waiting for: the U.S. stock market crashed.

Economic failure reverberated across the globe. An estimated 4.5 million people in Germany became unemployed. And while the Great Depression opened up certain highways for the Nazi Party, Hitler still had to overcome the existing powers. But thanks to their own failures, the road became far too accessible.

During Hindenburg's term as president, seven chancellors circulated below him. On March 27, 1930, Hermann Müller resigned as chancellor, replaced by Heinrich Brüning who likewise proved incapable. With disastrous mistakes of the sitting leadership, the gates began to fly open.

WINNING PARLIAMENT, WINNING GERMANY

While the president and chancellor played large roles in opening the doors for Hitler, he could not have come to power without the Reichstag. The September 1930 election of the German Parliament was a significant public advancement for the Nazis. The people were desperate, and Hitler's broad promises were just what they wanted to hear. According to The History Place, he appealed to all classes of Germans:

> Hitler offered something to everyone: work to the unemployed; prosperity to failed business people; profits to industry; expansion to the Army; social harmony and an end of class distinctions to ideal-istic young students; and restoration of German glory to those in despair. He promised to bring order amid chaos; a feeling of unity to all and the chance to belong. He would make Germany strong again; end payment of war reparations to the Allies; tear up the Treaty of Versailles; stamp out corruption; keep down Marxism; and deal harshly with the Jews. [6]

Overnight the Party went from holding a mere 12 seats to winning 107—making them the second largest group represented. Just as significantly, the votes didn't flow heavily from one sector of society, but came piling in from all directions—the working class, middle class, and the wealthy industrialists. As to be expected, with the victory new members came to join the Nazi Party in large waves. What had once been considered a fringe political group was now a dominating, socially accepted, and politically viable option. Germany's average Joes could join without worrying about causing a ruffle.

This was a substantial victory, and Hitler dug his heels in further for the fight, following the adage, "After a victory, fasten on the helmet more tightly." To increase the momentum, there was a frenzy of new gatherings popping up around the country—70,000 opportunities to storm towns for the Hitler cult. With relentless passion, the Nazis seized their opportunity.

And while the Party grew in notoriety, so did Hitler. The parliament success had not only made him a household name, but given him worldwide recognition. And as his reputation traversed continents and heightened, so too did his conceit and suspicion. The more people knew him, the more remote he grew. In every aspect of life, he proceeded with an arms-length distrust. He addressed nearly everyone by their surnames and discussed the issues he deemed important only with select individuals. Any disruption or disagreement and a person would be ousted, Hitler keeping detailed tabs of detractors with personal notes to handle them later. His focus was clear: it was no longer about elevating the state; it was about elevating himself.

The Nazi Party was divided between those who worshiped Hitler unceasingly and those who were loyal but questioned his means. Gregor Strasser in one breath worried about Hitler's long-lasting appeal to the public—"He doesn't smoke, he doesn't drink, he eats almost nothing but green stuff, he doesn't touch any woman! How are we supposed to understand him to put him across to other people?"[7] —while in the next admired his genius—"Whatever there is about him that is unpleasant, the man has a prophetic talent for reading great political problems correctly and doing the right thing at the opportune moment despite apparently insuperable difficulties."[8]

One of the reasons for Party members' distrust was likely Hitler's inability to truly steer the growing party. As enraptured as he was with being "The Leader," and as effective as he was in the public arena, he was evasive, inaccessible, and as undisciplined as he was in his youth. He took little notice of who he was leading or how his plans were being implemented and he avoided making decisions unless he felt compelled. One moment he was domineering and adamant; in the next he couldn't be found. Like the speeches and promises he made, the wrapping was appealing, but the meat was missing.

"This extraordinary way of operating was certainly built into Hitler's personality," wrote Kershaw. "Masterful and domineering, but uncertain and hesitant; unwilling to take decisions, yet then prepared to take decisions bolder than anyone else could contemplate; and refusal, once made, to take back any decision: these are part of the puzzle of Hitler's strange personality."[9] It was a lethal combination that, while contributing to his success, ultimately contributed far more to his personal and professional demise.

The next political milestone for the Nazis occurred in 1932. President Hindenburg's seven-year term was due to expire on May 5, and while this presented an ideal opportunity for Hitler to make his stand as ultimate leader, it would require him to run against the still greatly admired World War I hero.

Likewise, there was still the small issue of Hitler's citizenship. Despite it all, he was not a German citizen—a requirement to hold office. On February

26, to resolve the issue, Hitler acquired German citizenship by swearing an oath and becoming a civil servant. All the while, the Nazi propaganda continued at full tilt, and the Party was hopeful that this would be the year. But ultimately on election day in March, Hindenburg captured 49 percent of the vote to Hitler's 30 percent—shy of the required majority. In an April 10 runoff election, Hitler increased his share of the vote to 36 percent, but Hindenburg again pulled away victory, garnering 53 percent. The people stayed with their hero, and Hitler would have to wait for another occasion.

Inevitably, while Hitler would come to power legally, it would not be a personal vote that would put him into office. Instead, the Nazi Party would gain ultimate leverage in parliament, allowing Hitler and his influential friends to strong-arm a deal.

On July 31, 1932, the Nazis earned 230 seats out of 608, making them the largest represented party in parliament. While Hitler had lost the presidency, this was a large bargaining chip. With the people behind him, he felt entitled to the most prominent leadership role in the German state. Conferencing with President Hindenburg and Chancellor Franz von Papen, who had been in office only two months, Hitler demanded no less than "the leadership of the state to its full extent for himself and his party"[10]—among many other demands, he wanted to be appointed chancellor. But the meeting with Hindenburg lasted only twenty minutes, and the president did not find Hitler's entitlement so compelling. He told Hitler such an arrangement would not be possible, but instead offered to name Hitler vice-chancellor in a coalition government. Hitler declined the offer. He was then cautioned that any acts of treachery or subversion against the standing government would be pursued and handled ruthlessly. Hitler had been rejected. He had gambled and lost and been warned to stand down. What should have been widespread victory with the overtaking of parliament was now a crumpling defeat. But it would only be a matter of five months before 13 million individuals were officially under the thumb of the great Führer.

As expected, Hitler did not take defeat gracefully. With all the poise of an adolescent, he converted his disappointment and embarrassment into aggression, faulting the standing government in all their actions to try to bolster his self-image. Instead of admitting his personal rejection, he twisted the situation into his rejection of the government: "Those of you who possess a feel for the struggle for the honour and freedom of the nation," he said, "will understand why I refused to enter this bourgeois government. With this deed, our attitude towards this national cabinet is prescribed once and for all."[11]

Hitler's rejection had caused a political stalemate, and his plans were now in jeopardy. The public was growing weary of elections and the Nazi Party's inability to substantially penetrate the government. The middle class, which had been the meat of the party for so long, was losing its loyalty. If it weren't for Hitler's friends in influential positions, his road would have reached a dead-end.

The months between August 1932 and January 1933 were some of the most trying and uncertain for the Nazi Party. Hitler laid out his cards, determining he would be no part of a government if he were not granted the chancellorship. He hoped the threat of a Nazi revolution with its strong, unyielding numbers would force President Hindenburg to bow to his request. But Hindenburg had reservations—not only about the Party's direction, but more so about Hitler. Yielding to Hitler would be handing over democracy, cutting hope off at the knees. Hindenburg was not fooled by Hitler's rhetoric as so many others were. But von Papen believed Hitler could be more easily controlled from the inside and convinced Hindenburg to bring Hitler in as chancellor, with von Papen as vice-chancellor. Weary of the government stalemate and political infighting, the eighty-five-year-old president felt he simply had no other choice. And so when Hindenburg was forced to swear in the new chancellor on January 30, 1933, he could offer no words of congratulations or excitement. Instead he said only, "And now, gentlemen, forwards with God."[12]

It had taken over a decade, but Hitler finally had a position of power within Germany's government. An ecstatic Goebbels wrote in his diary that night: "It is almost like a dream...a fairytale...The new [Third] Reich has been born. Fourteen years of work have been crowned with victory. The German revolution has begun!"[13] And as Kershaw points out, Hitler's revolutionary agenda had hardly been veiled: "Whatever the avowals of following a legal path to power, heads would roll, he had said. Marxism would be eradicated, he had said. Jews would be 'removed,' he had said. Germany would rebuild the strength of its armed forces, destroy the shackles of Versailles, conquer 'by the sword' the land it needed for its 'living space,' he had said."[14] But few actually took him at his word.

THE NEW CHANCELLOR

With the fox now in the henhouse, Hitler immediately went to work to gain absolute power over Germany.

On his first day he convinced Hindenburg to dissolve the current parliament and call for new elections. With a Nazi majority elected to the Reichstag, they would readily approve whatever laws Hitler wanted.

At the same time, it is believed that Hitler's men came up with a plan to burn down the Reichstag building, blaming the Communists and fabricating tales of a Communist takeover plot. Whether they set the fire, or an arsonist did, they certainly exploited it. By creating a sense of chaos and panic, and playing on people's fears of communism, Hitler had no trouble convincing the aging president to sign an emergency decree to "protect the state."

Signed on February 28, the Law for the Protection of the People and the State suspended the sections of the Constitution relating to personal liberties:

> Restrictions on personal liberty, on the right of free expression of opinion, including freedom of the press; on the rights of assembly and association; and violations of the privacy of postal, telegraphic and telephonic communications; and warrants for house searches, orders for confiscations as well as restrictions on property, are also permissible beyond the legal limits otherwise prescribed.[15]

In the days leading up to the March 5 election, thousands of Nazi opponents—not just Communists but Social Democrats and others—were rounded up and arrested. Several dozen were killed. Anything deemed to be harmful to the government was prohibited, meaning that merely campaigning against the Nazis was now illegal. When the election was held, not surprisingly, the Nazi Party garnered 44 percent of the vote—not enough for a two-thirds majority, but enough to allow Hitler to continue virtually unchecked. One final law, passed by the new Reichstag, was the last nail in the coffin of democracy: the so-called Enabling Act changed the constitution to give Hitler the power to enact laws. With the passage of this Act on March 23, Adolf Hitler effectively became the dictator of Germany.

In his new position, Hitler used his powers to ensure the success of the Nazi Party.

He decreed that after July 14, 1933, the Nazis would become the only legal party in Germany. He disbanded all other organizations, and individual German states lost their autonomy as Nazi officials were established as governors and local police were replaced with Nazi officers. He banned labor unions and strikes, and he took control of universities, writers, and publishers. Architecture and modern art were forbidden, and certain literature (democratic, socialist, and Jewish) was blacklisted and burned by students and professors in the public squares.

And while these were no doubt drastic changes that could easily have lost the favor of the people, Hitler was a master manipulator and propagandist. After becoming chancellor, he was easily able to sway the German people. But apart from hollow propaganda, Hitler won the populace through effective economic reform. Large public programs helped to lift Germany up from the depression. Hitler made good on his pledge of "work and bread"[16] by building autobahns (highways), enormous sports stadiums, office buildings, and public housing. By 1938, businesses' profits greatly increased, and the standard of living for an average employee also improved.

Göetz Aly, a well-respected German historian and guest lecturer at Frankfurt University, wrote that Hitler was a "feel-good dictator."[17] According to German journalist Jody K. Biehl, Aly's book *Hitler's People's State* describes Hitler as "a leader who not only made Germans feel important, but also made sure they were well cared-for by the state. To do so, he gave them huge tax breaks and introduced social benefits that even today anchor the society. He also ensured that even in the last days of the war not a single German went hungry. Despite near-constant warfare, never once during his twelve years in power did Hitler raise taxes for working class people. He also—in great contrast to World War I—particularly pampered soldiers and their families, offering them more than double the salaries and benefits that American and British families received. As such, most Germans saw Nazism as a 'warm-hearted' protector. They were only too happy to overlook the Third Reich's unsavory, murderous side." How many realized—or cared—that this wealth would come primarily from robbing the Jews and plundering neighboring lands?[18]

When President Hindenburg died on August 2, 1934, Hitler's consolidation of power was complete. While Hindenburg's last wish had been to restore the monarchy, Hitler was (not surprisingly) unwilling to abide. The president's death allowed Hitler to combine the head of state with the leadership of government, abolishing the title of president and making himself Führer (supreme leader) and Reich (realm) Chancellor. The army pledged support to him personally, and with that there was no turning back. War, genocide, and the destruction of the homeland were all that loomed in the future.

· 4 ·

NATIONALISM, EXPANSIONISM, AND WAR

"The Führer gave expression to his unshakable
conviction that the Reich will be the master of all
Europe. We shall yet have to engage in many fights,
but these will undoubtedly lead to most wonderful
victories. From there on the way to world domination
is practically certain. Whoever dominates Europe will
thereby assume the leadership of the world."[1]

~ Joseph Goebbels, May 8, 1943

*U*NDERSTANDING HITLER'S motivations and objectives is essential to understanding his character. By the time Hindenburg died and the chancellorship and presidency were merged, giving Hitler total power, a new world was opened—one in which Hitler's objectives could be more directly pursued and understood.

But as we've seen in Hitler throughout the course of his life, he lived in his own reality. *Mein Kampf* was filled with Hitler's plans for Germany—plans that seemed outlandish and impractical. Traditionally there is a necessary distinction between the statesman and the full-tilt political trailblazer. Those who had read and understood Hitler's goals in *Mein Kampf* hoped that once he took the full reins of power there would be a degree of compromise and practicality. But it was never in Hitler's lifeblood to be practical.

Norman Rich, author of *Hitler's War Aims: Ideology, the Nazi State, and the Course of Expansion*, aptly observed, "Besides being a fanatic ideologue, Hitler was a pathological egotist whose lust for power and dominion expanded with the prospects that opened before him, often in defiance of all the rules he himself had laid down for the conduct of policy."[2]

THE NAZI PROPAGANDA MACHINE

Before we delve into Hitler's objectives, it's essential to understand how he came to a position where these objectives were even potential realities. Hitler's success would not have been possible without two things:

1) The vulnerability of the German state and people as we have previously discussed, and *2)* The Nazi propaganda machine.

Propaganda was a tremendous asset to Hitler, and his mastery of it allowed him to fully exploit the vulnerability of the people he claimed to serve. The propaganda mission was twofold. It needed to convince the current populace that Nazism provided the answers they were seeking. Secondly, the propaganda needed to create a sustainable claw that could dig deeply into the future generations.

As we look at propaganda, we need to consider what the term meant in the Nazi Party. In common terms, propaganda is the art of influence. It's convincing others, through effective persuasion, that what you believe and support is right. Propaganda often carries a negative connotation as it's often trying to convince people by appealing to their emotions rather than their mind. Propaganda is rarely about presenting the facts, but rather about presenting the most compelling—even if untrue—case.

In the Third Reich, propaganda took an extreme and dangerous form. Rather than limiting themselves to lies and manipulation of information, the Nazi Party would infiltrate whatever institution they wished to sway and physically remove any opposition members, killing them if necessary.

As Hitler was aware, "by an able and persistent use of propaganda heaven itself can be presented to the people as if it were hell and, vice versa, the most miserable kind of life can be presented as if it were paradise."[3]

It was the job of Dr. Joseph Goebbels, the Minister of Propaganda and National Enlightenment, to ensure that no citizen of Nazi Germany was privy to any information or campaigns that could be damaging to Hitler or the Party. Secondly, he had to promote the Nazi agenda, spinning a prejudiced, dangerous scheme in a manner that the population would not only allow but embrace.

In his own words, the danger of these two goals is apparent: "The essence of propaganda consists in winning people over to an idea so sincerely, so vitally, that in the end they succumb to it utterly and can never escape from it."

Essential to the Nazi propaganda machine were the SS (Hitler's personal guard) and Gestapo ("Secret State Police"). These two arms of the Third Reich were able to physically pursue and shut down the dissemination of information deemed damaging to the regime. By intimidation and brute force, they were able to lock out Hitler's opposition. Likewise, in 1933 Goebbels was able to establish the Reich Chamber of Commerce which officiated the production and availability of a variety of arts, including literature, music, radio programming, newspaper articles, etc. By creating a conduit of approval, Goebbels and his team could censor what contents were available to the public.

In conjunction with the new censorship came the great burnings. Goebbels organized public burnings of any publications that did not align with the Nazi mission. Among those were books by the German writer Heinrich Heine who aptly commented, "Where they burn books, so too will they in the end burn human beings."

Another instrumental act on the part of Goebbels was the creation and distribution of affordable radios called "The People's Receiver." Since the Nazis controlled the airwaves, Goebbels thought it important that as many people as possible be able to afford to hear the speeches of the Führer as well as other Nazi propaganda.

Further, the propaganda arm created massive public gatherings and rallies to bring together the population. Loud speakers were erected in the streets and public squares so individuals could hear—and were forced to hear—Hitler's message.

Goebbels even went so far as to build gigantic arenas to hold the tremendous rallies, lighting them up so the Nazi gathering could be seen from more than one hundred miles away.

Aside from these general measures, Hitler knew that if he won the hearts of the German youth, he would eventually win the nation, making his objectives viable for the long term. At the end of 1933, his youth programs had already enlisted over 3.5 million boys from ages six to eighteen and girls ages ten and older. By 1935, their members would eventually include about 60 percent of Germany's children. As we know, teen years are often the most influential; peer pressure is stronger than ever and malleable minds are easy to shape. Hitler knew his influence had to supersede all others, even the children's own parents. It was a form of indoctrination that could produce devastating results, as children were taught to report their parents or teachers if they seemed to be disloyal to the Reich.

For the adult population, Goebbels implemented a number of techniques to sway them to Nazi thinking, including fear of potential uprisings (Jewish, Slavic, Bolshevist); presenting an inaccurate portrayal of foreign (Allied) attitudes; and the constant rallying for national unity and economic strength. After being appointed chancellor, Hitler's first speech to the nation is a clear picture of his power of persuasion:

> During fourteen years the German nation has been at the mercy of decadent elements which have abused its confidence. During fourteen years those elements have done nothing but destroy, disintegrate, and dissolve. Hence it is neither temerity nor presumption if, appearing before the nation today, I ask: German nation, give us four years time, after which you can arraign us before your tribunal and you can judge me!...I cannot rid myself of my faith in my people, nor lose the conviction that this people will resuscitate again one day. I cannot be severed from the love of a people that I know to be my own. And I nourish the conviction that the hour will come when millions of men who now curse us will take their stand behind us to welcome the new Reich, our common creation born of a painful and laborious struggle and an arduous triumph—a Reich which is the symbol of greatness, honour, strength, honesty, and justice.[4]

One of Hitler's greatest propaganda achievements, though, was the Nazi treatment of Christianity. In Part Two as we discuss the Jewish question and Hitler's manipulation of the church, we'll take a closer look at his use of propaganda in its most effective and harmful setting.

REEDUCATION OF THE GERMAN PEOPLE

From the start, a number of Hitler's motivations stemmed from a hatred rather than a hope. He denied any value in the political notions governing Western society, finding fault with democracy as well as communism. He believed these poor systems and their faulty leaders had produced an overall degeneracy—one that had invaded Germany's borders, stunting the population's potential. Reeducation was therefore a necessity, as citizens would need to learn and adopt the values of a Nazi Germany. The Third Reich claimed the slogan "Germany Awake"—a deliberate call to cast off the clothing of a defeated nation and once again claim its place as a world power with an elite society.

"The law of the National Socialist Revolution has yet to run its course," Hitler said, addressing a group of Nazi leaders in the summer of 1933. "Its dynamic force still dominates development in Germany today, a development which presses forward irresistibly to a complete remodeling of German life...Just as a magnet draws from a composite mass only the steel chips, so should a movement directed exclusively towards political struggle draw to itself only those natures which are called to political leadership...The German Revolution will not be complete until the whole German people has been fashioned anew, until it has been organized anew and has been reconstructed."

But with Germany, as with any society, there was a prevailing first class that was accustomed to pulling the levers and being the influential few. For Nazi philosophy to take hold, this system would have to change, fundamentally reorganizing German society to a state of uniformity, encouraging a new sense of national harmony that would dominate all else.

The national community, referred to as Volksgemeinschaft, was reinforced continually with propaganda. People were taught to put the group before the individual, and they were continually subjected to the refrain: "One people! One Reich! One Führer!" Hitler was to be seen as the messiah—the religious connotation highly important—who would lead the society back to its glorious roots. He was presented as a selfless character who cared only about the people.

"In the years leading up to the war—partly as an antidote to the increasing use of coercion and for the subsequent loss of liberty, propaganda eulogized the achievements of the regime," wrote David Welch in his book *Hitler*. "The press, radio, newsreels and film documentaries concentrated on the more prominent schemes...Posters proclaimed the benefits of 'Socialism of the Deed,' newsreels showed happy workers enjoying cruise holidays and visiting the 'People's Theatre' for the first time, the radio bombarded the public's social conscience with charitable appeals, and the press stressed the value of belonging to a 'national community' and the need for self-sacrifice in the interests of the state. The intention was to move away from social confrontation towards conciliation and integration."[5]

In addition, the Third Reich mandated more public holidays and public customs that brought the community together under one umbrella. The more positive, group-affirming scenarios the regime could enact, the more likely the masses were to line up willingly behind the Führer.

Propaganda was shouting the virtues of the Nazi Party from the rooftops. And while it was effective at convincing a significant number, the rest of the citizens were kept in line by fear and repression. Through brutal and constant intimidation, the Nazis convicted 12,000 Germans of high treason between 1933 and 1939. When the war began, another 15,000 were added into the tortuous mix and handed the ultimate punishment.

EXPANSIONISM AND WAR

While ensuring that Germany was on course to eliminate the subordinate races and become a united, ethnically cleansed national community was extremely important to Hitler, he had an utter fascination with foreign policy. Hitler's goal ultimately was to establish a new order of absolute German power across continental Europe. His foreign policy relied heavily on expansionism and gaining Lebensraum ("living space") for the Aryan race.

While Hitler had certainly mentioned the key need for expansion throughout his rise to power, his goals for living space were detailed more explicitly in a November 5, 1937, meeting with his chiefs of staff. Hitler expressed his belief that Germany had an implied right to a greater living space and that "the only remedy, and one which might seem visionary, is the acquisition of a greater living space—a quest that has in every age been the origin of the formation of states and the migration of peoples."

In order for Germany to expand, however, Hitler would need to remove the obstacles of the Treaty of Versailles. Again, propaganda was Hitler's chief ally. The dictator was able to far too easily convince the nations he was standing against Bolshevism. In

October 1933, the Nazis withdrew Germany from the Geneva Disarmament Conference and from the League of Nations, alarming Italy as well as France and Britain. But with every drastic move, Hitler also countered with the band-aid of a fresh agreement, insisting Germany was only removing the unfair regulations in the towering treaty, giving the new growing country room to be a more effective ally to its European nations. In January 1934, Hitler signed a nonaggression treaty with Poland and in June 1935, a naval treaty with Britain. Perhaps most crucial, though, was when he was able to remilitarize the Rhineland in spring of 1936 thanks to a pact between France and the Soviet Union. In 1936, Hitler established key allies in Italy and Japan, and in 1937 he began laying out his plans for controversial expansion to his military leaders.

The first major military conquest was in February 1938 when Germany invaded Austria. A free country in 1933, a year later Austria's government began to centralize its power and welcomed influential Nazi sympathizers. By 1938 it was a Nazi dictatorship.

With more than 30 percent unemployment, 25% inflation, and general unrest, the Austrian people longed for someone to rescue them from their economic and political turmoil. When Hitler campaigned in Austria and promised to solve their problems if they were annexed to Germany, they were taken in by his power of persuasion. He offered them hope, and quickly won them over. They didn't see him as we do today: as a cruel, arrogant man with bloodied hands. Rather they saw him as a friendly and caring figure, with outstretched hands in a time of national trouble.

In "My Patient, Hitler," published in March 1941 in Collier's Weekly, Dr. Eduard Bloch, the Hitler family doctor, gives insight into Austria's reaction to the Führer:

> On Friday, March 11, 1938, the Vienna radio was broadcasting a program of light music. It was 7:45 at night. Suddenly the announcer broke in. The chancellor would speak. Schuschnigg came on the air and said that to prevent bloodshed he was capitulating to the wishes of Hitler. The frontiers would be opened; he ended his address with the words: "Gott schiitze Oesterreich" — May God protect Austria. Hitler was coming home to Linz.
>
> In the sleepless days that followed we clung to our radios. Troops were pouring over the border at Passau, Kufstein, Mittenwalde and elsewhere. Hitler himself was crossing the Inn River at Braunau, his birthplace. Breathlessly, the announcer told us the story of the march. The Fuehrer himself would pause in Linz. The

town went mad with joy. The reader should have no doubts about the popularity of Anschluss [union] with Germany. The people favored it. They greeted the onrushing tide of German troops with flowers, cheers and songs. Church bells rang. Austrian troops and police fraternized with the invaders and there was general rejoicing.

The public square in Linz, a block from my home, was a turmoil. All afternoon it rang with the Horst Wessel song and Deutschland über Alles [German national anthem, "Germany Above All"]. Planes droned overhead, and advance units of the German army were given deafening cheers.[6]

After being annexed, Austria would see new government jobs created by Hitler and prosperity return to the nation. But the honeymoon wouldn't last for long. One Austrian remembers:

I lived in Austria under Adolf Hitler's regime for seven years. Dictatorship did not happen overnight. It was a gradual process starting with national identification cards, which we had to carry with us at all times...Gun registration followed, with a lot of talk about gun safety and hunting accidents...Freedom of speech was the next target...With a large network of informers, people were afraid to say anything political, even in their own homes.[7]

Hitler's aim was world domination, and Austria was only the beginning. With a swift and nearly resistanceless occupation, Hitler's inflated sense of capability only heightened. Following his triumph, he demanded the Sudetenland areas, inhabited by ethnic Germans, from the Czechoslovakian government. Thinking they could appease a tyrant, Britain, France, and Italy signed the Munich Agreement in September 1938, forcing the Czech government to hand them over. Though British Prime Minister Neville Chamberlain warned that if Germany invaded Poland there would be war in Europe, he returned home and naïvely proclaimed there would be "peace in our time."[8] But shortly thereafter, German troops invaded the rest of Czechoslovakia, followed by Lithuania.

It was only a matter of time before someone was going to have to stand up to Hitler's pickpocketing ways. His lust for expansionism was not to be satisfied, and with his current progress unimpeded, he felt only more capable of his potential.

Despite what had seemed like the complete impracticality of his goals in *Mein Kampf*, Hitler followed them with sincere and relentless audacity. Suspecting he might have to face a two-front battle with Russia in the east, and Britain and France in the west, in August 1939 Hitler negotiated a nonaggression pact with Stalin, his archenemy. Their private accord was to divide Poland between Germany and the Soviet Union, and with that Hitler invaded Poland on September 1, 1939. Unable to pacify the dictator, France and Britain knew what they had to do and quickly declared war on the overreaching German state.

A WORLD AT WAR

World War II came to be the deadliest conflict in human history, resulting in the deaths of an estimated 50–70 million individuals. Most of Europe lay in ruins, and millions became homeless refugees. Over its six-year span, the war came to involve the major world powers, separating them into military alliances called the Allies (namely the United Kingdom, the Soviet Union, and the United States) and the Axis (namely Germany, Italy, and Japan).

In the first years, 1939–1941, Germany conquered or suppressed a large portion of Europe, and the Axis powers seemed to easily be slipping into a position of domination. In the summer of 1941, they invaded the Soviet Union, proving themselves to be the fearless, if not irrational, pawns of Hitler. In December, Japan attacked the United States and many European posts in the Pacific Ocean.

But 1942 saw the tables turn. Japan was defeated in a series of naval battles, and the Axis powers were stopped dead in their tracks at Stalingrad. By 1943, after numerous Allied invasions and victories across Europe and the Pacific, the Axis powers were forced to retreat. In 1944, Germany was compelled to turn inward even further, their own land invaded by the Soviet Union. The Allied troops were closing in on Berlin and the end of the Nazi reign.

MASS SUICIDES IN 1945

As it became clear the war was coming to a close in 1945 and the Nazi mission would not succeed, count-less individuals, including high-ranking Nazi officials, committed suicide. Many of those still felt loyal to the Führer and his mission. Indeed, there was a Nazi cult of death that had bound themselves to their own demise. And yet some of the suicides were executed for an entirely different reason: shame. At the culmi-nation of an era, a number of people began to realize the utter degradation and sin of which they were a part. With the Allies coming to occupy Germany and the aftermath that would occur, some simply could not stomach being publicly exposed for the atrocities they supported. *Life* magazine published an in-depth article about the suicides, noting, "In the last days of the war the overwhelming realization of utter defeat was too much for many Germans. Stripped of the bayonets and bombast which had given them power, they could not face a reckoning with either their conquerors or their consciences. These found the quickest and surest escape in what Germans call selbstmord, self-murder."[9]

While suicide seems a drastic measure, it is in tune with the Third Reich's concept of no compromise. It would either be success the Nazi way, or no success at all. For as long as the Nazis had been in power, they had endorsed extremes, and the end would be no different.

Hitler began promoting his stance on this as early as September 1939 when German forces were invading Poland. Before the Reichstag he said, "I now wish to be nothing other than the first soldier of the German Reich. Therefore I have put on that tunic which has always been the most holy and dear to me. I shall not take it off again until after victory is ours, or—I shall not live to see the day!"

As it became more and more apparent that Germany would not be the victors, propaganda filtered throughout Germany endorsing the glorious and honorable prospect of taking one's life. Radio broadcasts boasted of the dignity, and pamphlets recounted the noble suicides of Germans from the past. Hitler passed out cyanide pills to his staff, as they were told there were only two choices: triumph or ruin. Throughout 1945, 7,057 suicides were reported in Berlin.

In the end, Hitler and his key staff members were among those who chose the path of "ultimate sacrifice"—including Joseph Goebbels, Heinrich Himmler, and Martin Bormann.

On April 29, very early in the morning, Hitler married Eva Braun, his longtime companion. Shortly afterward, he went with his secretary, Traudl Junge, to a separate room and dictated his last will and testament. Hans Krebs, Wilhelm Burgdorf, Goebbels, and Bormann all served as witnesses to these documents, which explicitly detailed Hitler's and his new wife's pact of suicide. The following day, April 30, 1945, Soviet troops were closing in, and, as promised, Hitler and his new bride committed suicide, by pistol and cyanide capsule, respectively. His will and testament provide an insightful look into the mind of Hitler in his final hours.

Goebbels was one of those most disheartened by the loss of Hitler. Upon learning of Hitler's suicide, he said, "The heart of Germany has ceased to beat. The

Führer is dead."[10] While Hitler had asked Goebbels to continue on and lead the government, he couldn't find it within himself to continue and dictated an addendum to Hitler's testament:

> The Führer has given orders for me, in case of a breakdown of defense of the Capital of the Reich, to leave Berlin and to participate as a leading member in a government appointed by him. For the first time in my life, I must categorically refuse to obey a command of the Führer. My wife and my children agree with this refusal. In any other case, I would feel myself...a dishonorable renegade and vile scoundrel for my entire further life, who would lose the esteem of himself along with the esteem of his people, both of which would have to form the requirement for further duty of my person in designing the future of the German Nation and the German Reich.[11]

On May 1, Goebbels had his six children injected with morphine. Once unconscious, each was fed cyanide to end his or her lives. Immediately afterward, Goebbels and his wife retired to the garden of the Chancellery and committed suicide.

THE PRIVATE AND POLITICAL
TESTAMENTS OF HITLER

MY PRIVATE WILL AND TESTAMENT

As I did not consider that I could take responsibility, during the years of struggle, of con-
tracting a marriage, I have now decided, before
the closing of my earthly career, to take as my
wife that girl who, after many years of faithful
friendship, entered, of her own free will, the
practically besieged town in order to share her
destiny with me. At her own desire she goes as
my wife with me into death. It will compensate
us for what we both lost through my work in the
service of my people.

What I possess belongs—insofar as it has any
value—to the Party. Should this no longer exist, to
the State; should the State also be destroyed, no
further decision of mine is necessary.

My pictures, in the collections which I have
bought in the course of years, have never been
collected for private purposes, but only for the
extension of a gallery in my home town of Linz
a.d. Donau.

It is my most sincere wish that this bequest
may be duly executed.

I nominate as my Executor my most faithful
Party comrade, Martin Bormann

He is given full legal authority to make all
decisions. He is permitted to take out everything
that has a sentimental value or is necessary for

the maintenance of a modest simple life, for my brothers and sisters, also above all for the mother of my wife and my faithful co-workers who are well known to him, principally my old Secretaries Frau Winter, etc., who have for many years aided me by their work.

I myself and my wife—in order to escape the disgrace of deposition or capitulation—choose death. It is our wish to be burnt immediately on the spot where I have carried out the greatest part of my daily work in the course of twelve years' service to my people.

Given in Berlin, 29th April 1945, 4:00 o'clock

~ *A. Hitler*[12]

MY POLITICAL TESTAMENT

More than thirty years have now passed since I in 1914 made my modest contribution as a volunteer in the first world-war that was forced upon the Reich.

In these three decades I have been actuated solely by love and loyalty to my people in all my thoughts, acts, and life. They gave me the strength to make the most difficult decisions which have ever confronted mortal man. I have spent my time, my working strength, and my health in these three decades.

It is untrue that I or anyone else in Germany wanted the war in 1939. It was desired and instigated exclusively by those international statesmen who were either of Jewish descent or worked for Jewish interests. I have made too many offers for the control and limitation of armaments, which posterity will not for all time be able to disregard, for the responsibility for the outbreak of this war to be laid on me. I have further never wished that after the first fatal world war a second against England, or even against America, should break out. Centuries will pass away, but out of the ruins of our towns and monuments the hatred against those finally responsible whom we have to thank for everything, international Jewry and its helpers, will grow.

Three days before the outbreak of the German-Polish war I again proposed to the British ambassador in Berlin a solution to the German-Polish problem—similar to that in the case of the Saar district, under international control. This offer also cannot be denied. It was only rejected because the leading circles in English politics wanted the war, partly on account of the business hoped for and partly under influence of propaganda organized by international Jewry.

I have also made it quite plain that, if the nations of Europe are again to be regarded as mere shares to be bought and sold by these international conspirators in money and finance, then that race, Jewry, which is the real criminal of this murderous struggle, will be saddled with the responsibility. I further left no one in doubt that this time not only would millions of children of Europe's Aryan peoples die of hunger, not only would millions of grown men suffer death, and not only hundreds of thousands of women and children be burnt and bombed to death in the towns, without the real criminal having to atone for this guilt, even if by more humane means.

After six years of war, which in spite of all set-backs will go down one day in history as the most glorious and valiant demonstration of a nation's life purpose, I cannot forsake the city which is the capital of this Reich. As the forces are too small to make any further stand against the enemy attack at this place and our resistance is gradually being weakened by men who are as deluded as they are lacking in initiative, I should like, by remaining in this town, to share my fate with those, the millions of others, who have also taken upon themselves to do so. Moreover I do not wish to fall into the hands of an enemy who requires a new spectacle organized by the Jews for the amusement of their hysterical masses.

I have decided therefore to remain in Berlin and there of my own free will to choose death at the moment when I believe the position of the Fuehrer and Chancellor itself can no longer be held.

I die with a happy heart, aware of the immeasurable deeds and achievements of our soldiers at the front, our women at home, the achievements of our farmers and workers and the work, unique in history, of our youth who bear my name.

That from the bottom of my heart I express my thanks to you all, is just as self-evident as my wish that you should, because of that, on no account give up the struggle, but rather continue it against the enemies of the Fatherland, no matter where, true to the creed of a great Clausewitz. From the sacrifice of our soldiers and from my own unity with them unto death, will in any case spring up in the history of Germany, the seed of a radiant renaissance of the National-Socialist movement and thus of the realization of a true community of nations.

Many of the most courageous men and women have decided to unite their lives with mine until the very last. I have begged and finally ordered them not to do this, but to take part in the further battle of the Nation. I beg the heads of the Armies, the Navy, and the Air Force to strengthen by all possible means the spirit of resistance of our soldiers in the National-Socialist sense, with special reference to the fact that also I myself, as founder and creator of this movement, have preferred death to cowardly abdication or even capitulation.

May it, at some future time, become part of the code of honour of the German officer—as is already the case in our Navy—that the surrender of a district or of a town is impossible, and that above all the leaders here must march ahead as shining examples, faithfully fulfilling their duty unto death.

SECOND PART OF THE POLITICAL TESTAMENT

Before my death I expel the former Reichsmarschall Hermann Goering from the party and deprive him of all rights which he may enjoy by virtue of the decree of June 29th, 1941; and also by virtue of my statement in the Reichstag on September 1st, 1939, I appoint in his place Grossadmiral Doenitz, President of the Reich and Supreme Commander of the Armed Forces.

Before my death I expel the former Reichs-fuehrer-SS and Minister of the Interior, Heinrich Himmler, from the party and from all offices of State. In his stead I appoint Gauleiter Karl Hanke as Reichsfuehrer-SS and Chief of the German Police, and Gauleiter Paul Giesler as Reich Minister of the Interior.

Goering and Himmler, quite apart from their disloyalty to my person, have done immeasurable harm to the country and the whole nation by secret negotiations with the enemy, which they conducted without my knowledge and against my wishes, and by illegally attempting to seize power in the State for themselves.

In order to give the German people a government composed of honourable men—a government which will fulfill its pledge to continue the war by every mean—I appoint the following members of the new Cabinet as leaders of the nation:

President of the Reich: DOENITZ

Chancellor of the Reich: DR. GOEBBELS

Party Minister: BORMANN

Foreign Minister: SEYSS-INQUART

[Here follow fifteen others.]

Although a number of these men, such as

Martin Bormann, Dr. Goebbels, etc., together with their wives, have joined me of their own free will and did not wish to leave the capital of the Reich under any circumstances, but were willing to perish with me here, I must nevertheless ask them to obey my request, and in this case set the interests of the nation above their own feelings. By their work and loyalty as comrades they will be just as close to me after death, as I hope that my spirit will linger among them and always go with them. Let them be hard, but never unjust, above all let them never allow fear to influence their actions, and set the honour of the nation above everything in the world. Finally, let them be conscious of the fact that our task, that of continuing the building of a National Socialist State, represents the work of the coming centuries, which places every single person under an obligation always to serve the common interest and to subordinate his own advantage to this end. I demand of all Germans, all National Socialists, men, women and all the men of the Armed Forces, that they be faithful and obedient unto death to the new government and its President.

Above all I charge the leaders of the nation and those under them to scrupulous observance of the laws of race and to merciless opposition to the universal poisoner of all peoples, international Jewry.

Given in Berlin, this 29th day of April 1945. 4:00 A.M.

~ *Adolf Hitler*[13]

Adolf Hitler poses with a young girl to whom he gives his autograph.
The above photo, and all photos on the following pages, courtesy of the United States Holocaust Memorial Museum.

ABOVE: Two Jews are executed by hanging in Olkusz.

RIGHT: A "wolf-cub" or junior member of the Hitler Youth hands Hitler a letter written by the child's sick mother.

OPPOSITE: German President Paul von Hindenburg rides in an open car with Adolf Hitler, the newly appointed Chancellor.

LEFT AND RIGHT: Jewish women and children are ordered to undress prior to their execution.

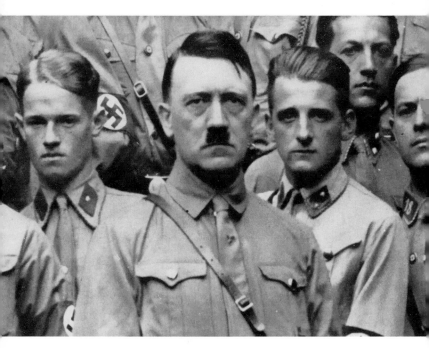

Adolf Hitler poses with a group of SS members soon after his appointment as Chancellor.

Hitler looks out of a train.

German police and auxiliaries in civilian clothes look on as a group of Jewish women are forced to undress before their execution.

A smiling Adolf Hitler greets a soldier. Pictured at the center with goggles is Hitler's aide-de-camp Heinz Linge.

A wagon is piled high with the bodies of former prisoners in the newly liberated Buchenwald Concentration Camp.

TOP: Jewish women from Subcarpathian Rus who have been selected for forced labor at Aschwitz-Birkenau, wait to be taken to another section of the camp.

ABOVE: Jewish women from Subcarpathian Rus who have been selected for forced labor at Aschwitz-Birkenau, march toward their barracks after disinfection and headshaving.

Adolf Hitler casts his vote at a Berlin polling station set up in a schoolroom.

Benito Mussolini and Adolf Hitler stand together on a reviewing stand during an official visit to occupied Yugoslavia.

Part 2

DISCOVERING RELIGION IN THE REICH

THE JEWISH QUESTION

"His is no master people; he is an exploiter: the
Jews are a people of robbers. He has never
founded any civilization, though he has destroyed
civilizations by the hundred."[1]

~ Adolf Hitler

WHILE IT'S OBVIOUS to see the result
of Hitler's hatred of the Jewish race,
exactly how it began is unknown.

In 1922 when Joseph Hell asked Hitler what he
intended doing if he ever had full freedom of action

against the Jews, his response was clear: "If I am ever really in power, the destruction of the Jews will be my first and most important job. As soon as I have power, I shall have gallows after gallows erected, for example, in Munich on the Marienplat—as many of them as traffic allows. Then the Jews will be hanged one after another, and they will stay hanging until they stink. They still stay hanging as long as hygienically possible. As soon as they are untied, then the next group will follow and that will continue until the last Jew in Munich is exterminated. Exactly the same procedure will be followed in other cities until Germany is cleansed of the last Jew!"[2]

But his hatred was not always so systematic and clear. In *Mein Kampf*, Hitler talked about growing up in Linz. There were some Jews whom he saw as being no different than other Germans. It wasn't until he was fourteen or fifteen years old that he "ran up against the word 'Jew,' partly in connection with political controversies."[3] He said that he had a slight aversion whenever he heard the word. Ironically, when he moved to Vienna he often dealt with Jewish businessmen, and he claimed to be put off by the anti-Semitism he read about in the Viennese press: "In the Jew I still saw only a man who was of a different religion, and, therefore, on grounds of human tolerance, I was against the idea that he should be attacked because he had a different faith. And so I considered that the tone adopted by the anti-Semitic press in Vienna was unworthy of the cultural traditions of a great people."[4]

These are hauntingly strange words from history's foremost anti-Semite. Something horrible must have taken place to so radically change Hitler's view of the Jewish people, but identifying a sole culprit is difficult. There are a number of factors that may have caused such a deep-rooted hatred that resulted in the murder of millions.

For starters, we have Hitler's inability to acknowledge personal failure. Throughout his life, he secured scapegoats to explain his deficiencies and disappointments. One of the primary disappointments prior to his introduction to politics was obviously his rejection from the Academy of Fine Arts in Vienna. When Hitler submitted his art, the deciding professors maintained that his paintings were unwanted because they had too few people in them. The examining board didn't want someone who was simply a landscape artist. Hitler didn't find this to be an adequate explanation. His art was worthy; there had to be a mitigating factor that could explain his rejection. Upon further research, Hitler found his culprit: four of the seven professors were Jewish. After this decided rejection and his spiral into poverty, Hitler found himself painting postcards and shoveling snow in a nice area of Vienna where a number of Jews lived. His resentment toward the Jews grew as he noted their success.

Reading *Mein Kampf*, it's easy to see evidence of this bitterness. He claimed his impoverished time in Vienna was entirely the fault of the Jews:

> But a Jew can never be rescued from his fixed notions. It was then simple enough to attempt to show them the absurdity of their teaching. Within my small circle I talked to them until my throat ached and my voice grew hoarse. I believed that I could finally convince them of the danger inherent in the Marxist follies. But I only achieved the contrary result...
>
> If your adversary felt forced to give in to your argument, on account of the observers present, and if you then thought that at last you had gained ground, a surprise was in store for you on the following day. The Jew would be utterly oblivious to what had happened the day before, and he would start once again by repeating his former absurdities, as if nothing had happened. Should you become indignant and remind him of yesterday's defeat, he pretended astonishment and could not remember anything, except that on the previous day he had proved that his statements were correct. Sometimes I

was dumbfounded. I do not know what amazed me more—the abundance of their verbiage or the artful way in which they dressed up their false-hoods. I gradually came to hate them.[5]

Another theory was that Hitler suffered from an advanced stage of syphilis. When he was in Vienna, he possibly contracted the disease from a Jewish prostitute. Some believe that this can be verified by comments Hitler made in *Mein Kampf*. According to Dr. Bassem Habeeb, a psychiatrist at Hollins Park Hospital Warrington, when you look at Hitler's life through the lens of a syphilis diagnosis, one clue leads to another until a pattern emerges of a mind and body ravaged by the disease. This theory would explain why Hitler devoted thirteen pages to the disease in *Mein Kampf*. The job of "combating syphilis...the Jewish disease...should be the task of the entire German nation," he wrote. "The health of the nation will be regained only by eliminating the Jews."[6]

If Hitler was truly wasting away physically and mentally because of syphilis and he contracted it from a Jewish prostitute, then it would explain why he focused on the disease so much. It might also explain why he became more vehement, to the degree of lunacy, in his hatred of the Jews.

A third potential factor is a simple one of human nature: jealousy. Much like his need for a scapegoat, Hitler fell victim to the common human foible of envy. World War I deeply destroyed Germany's economy, as well as its morale. As we witnessed in previous chapters, Hitler took the defeat of the German state very personally and could not cope with reactions from the populace that seemed to go against the grain of the nation. After the war when many Jews were resourceful and able to survive economically, a number of less resourceful and less fortunate Germans found it easy to resent their success. Embedded with a nationalistic rather than individual focus, Hitler was among those who found the Jews' prosperity, in a time of suffering, to be distasteful and selfish—further evidence of their truly inferior nature.

And while all of these reasons are understandable, if not accurate, one of the most compelling explanations of the origins of Hitler's anti-Semitism comes from the indoctrination and persuasion by outside influences—the individuals who sowed the seeds of hatred.

Several individuals helped to fuel Hitler's hatred for the Jewish people and contributed to the rise of anti-Semitism in Nazi Germany.

Henry Ford (1863–1947)

American automaker Henry Ford wrote a number of virulent anti-Semitic articles in his weekly paper, the *Dearborn Independent*. Under the banner "The International Jew: The World's Problem," Ford declared, "This people has ever been fouling the earth and plotting to dominate it. In order to eventually rule the Gentiles, the Jews have long been conspiring to form an international super-capitalist government." This racial problem, the *Independent* said, was the "prime" question confronting all society.[7]

These ninety-one articles were published in book form as *The International Jew*, and translated into German as *The Eternal Jew*. Ford's book was tremendously popular in Germany and became an effective piece of Nazi propaganda greatly influencing the people toward anti-Semitism.

An advocate of eugenics, Ford was convinced that the "German-Jewish bankers"—these "parasites, these sloths and lunatics...apostles of murder"—were responsible for society's ills, ideas that resonated well with Hitler's ideology.[8]

"I regard Henry Ford as my inspiration," Hitler told a Detroit News reporter two years before becoming the German chancellor in 1933, explaining why he kept a life-size portrait of the American automaker next to his desk.[9]

Hitler's office also held multiple copies of Ford's book, and some argue that Hitler went so far as to paraphrase many passages from Ford's writings in *Mein Kampf*. On his seventy-fifth birthday, Ford was awarded the Grand Cross of the German Eagle, Germany's highest honor, by his longtime admirer, the Führer.

Ford was extremely popular in the United States, and years after his articles were published, he issued an apology for his anti-Jewish sentiments. Most forgave him, but had he known the fire he was fueling in Germany, one must think that he would have at least kept his thoughts to himself.

Richard Wagner (1813–1883)

Hitler was known to say, "Whoever wants to understand National Socialist Germany must know Wagner."[10] And indeed, it's a telling point. When Hitler officially came to power in 1933, it was the fiftieth anniversary of the famous opera composer Richard Wagner's death, and this anniversary was celebrated throughout Germany under the premise "Wagner and the new Germany."

Wagner was well known for his anti-Semitism. At the age of thirty-seven he wrote Das Judentum in der Musik (Judaism in Music), in which he claimed Jews weren't equipped to be original or creative, and were "freaks of nature": "The Jew...no matter to what European nationality we belong has something disagreeably foreign to that nationality: instinctively we wish to have nothing in common with a man who looks like that."[11] Describing an "involuntary repellence,"[12] "instinctive dislike,"[13] and "natural repugnance against the Jewish nature,"[14] he claimed that the Jews ruled financially, and he therefore argued for the "necessity of fighting for emancipation from the Jews."[15]

In addition to anti-Semitism, his operas focused heavily on a violent and war-driven Germany, claiming Jesus was born a German and that the German people would soon awaken and take back their rightful place as the superior race. As a representative of high culture, he made anti-Semitism respectable.

In Wagner's *Hitler: The Prophet and His Disciple*, Ronald Taylor writes, "Time and again Wagner called for the annihilation of the Jewish race, an alien body in an Aryan German state. Hitler took him at his word."

Houston Chamberlain (1855–1927)

Perhaps one of the lesser-known contributors to the concept of racial supremacy was Houston Chamberlain, who later married composer Richard Wagner's daughter, Eva. He penned a book entitled *The Foundations of the Nineteenth Century* that would claim even the attention of Kaiser Wilhelm II—Germany's leader during World War I. Kaiser said, "It was God who sent your book to the German people and you personally to me."[17]

Such a statement is alarming given that Chamberlain believed deeply in the superiority of the Aryan race and the corrupt nature of the Jews. "Whoever claimed that Jesus was a Jew was either being stupid or telling a lie...Jesus was not a Jew," wrote Chamberlain. "He was probably an Aryan!"

Germany's loss following World War I caused Chamberlain extreme distress, but with Hitler's rise, his notions of German supremacy resurfaced. "My faith in Germanism has not wavered for an instant," he wrote Hitler. "With one stroke you have transformed the state of my soul. That Germany, in the hour of her greatest need, brings forth a Hitler—that is proof of her vitality...May God protect you!"[18]

When Chamberlain died in January 1927, Hitler attended his funeral, along with other members of the Nazi Party. The anti-Semitic concepts that Chamberlain expressed in *The Foundations* would prove to be guideposts for Hitler's regime.

Charles Darwin (1809–1882)

Charles Darwin, of course, was the propeller behind the concept of "survival of the fittest." Prior to Darwin, the Western world largely held to the biblical beliefs that all human life was sacred and that the weak and vulnerable were to be cared for and protected. Darwin's notion, plugged into the hands of someone like Hitler, led to social and political policies that allowed men to be "as cruel as nature"—a process of weeding out the inferior, which, in Germany's case, proved often to be the Jews.

In describing how natural selection affects civilized nations, Darwin wrote in *Descent of Man*:

> We civilized men...do our utmost to check the process of elimination; we build asylums for the imbecile, the maimed, and the sick; we institute poor-laws; and our medical men exert their utmost skill to save the life of every one to the last moment. There is reason to believe that vaccination has preserved thousands, who from a weak

constitution would formerly have succumbed to small-pox. Thus the weak members of civilized societies propagate their kind. No one who has attended to the breeding of domestic animals will doubt that this must be highly injurious to the race of man. It is surprising how soon a want of care, or care wrongly directed, leads to the degeneration of a domestic race; but excepting in the case of man himself, hardly any one is so ignorant as to allow his worst animals to breed.[19]

Hitler echoed Darwin's evolutionary philosophy and took it to its logical conclusions. For example, he wrote in *Mein Kampf*, "The demand that it should be made impossible for defective people to continue to propagate defective offspring is a demand that is based on most reasonable grounds, and its proper fulfilment is the most humane task that mankind has to face. Unhappy and undeserved suffering in millions of cases will be spared, with the result that there will be a gradual improvement in national health."[20]

In addition to preventing weak and defective individuals from reproducing, Hitler argued that weaker races should not breed with the stronger. "Every crossing between two breeds which are not quite equal results in a...biologically lower order of being" compared to the higher parent, and therefore, he reasoned, "it must eventually succumb in any struggle against the higher species. Such mating contradicts the will of Nature towards the selective improvements of life in general."[21] The solution, he suggests, is not to mate individuals of higher and lower orders of being but rather to allow the complete triumph of the higher order. The stronger must dominate and not mate with the weaker, which would signify the sacrifice of its own higher nature. If Nature does not wish that weaker individuals should mate with the stronger, she wishes even less that a superior race should intermingle with an inferior one; because in such a case all her efforts, throughout hundreds of thousands of years, to establish an evolutionary higher stage of being, may thus be rendered futile.[22]

In Hitler's mind there was no doubt who the stronger, superior race was:

> Every manifestation of human culture, every product of art, science and technical skill, which we see before our eyes to-day, is almost exclusively the product of the Aryan creative power. This very fact fully justifies the conclusion that it was the Aryan alone who founded a superior type of humanity; therefore he represents the archetype of what we understand by the term: MAN. He is the Prometheus of mankind, from whose shining brow the divine spark of genius has at all times flashed forth,...showing man how to rise and become master over all the other beings on the earth.[23]

Darwin's observation of the survival of the fittest in nature was interpreted to mean only the fittest should survive—and Hitler was happy to take Nature's place in ensuring that it was done. Hitler believed in an "inexorable law that it is the strongest and the best who must triumph and that they have the right to endure. He who would live must fight. He who does not wish to fight in this world, where permanent struggle is the law of life, has not the right to exist."[24]

In Hitler's view, the German people were the superior race that deserved to rule the world. The Nazis even created a list of superior races, with the Aryans at the top, and Jews, Gypsies, and blacks at the bottom. The evolutionary philosophies espoused by Charles Darwin were at the core of Hitler's ideology, and this belief in the superiority of the Aryan race motivated the Third Reich to implement the practices of eugenics, euthanasia, forced sterilization, and racial extermination. As Nazi leader Rudolf Hess admitted, "National Socialism is nothing but applied biology."[25]

Perhaps Hitler's hatred of the Jews stemmed from a number of causes—his bitter sense of rejection, jealousy, the political climate, the influences of others, etc. Knowing that the Bible says the Jews are

God's chosen people no doubt added to Hitler's hatred, because he believed the German people were the master race, superior to all others. Add in the fact that the Jews had a way of gaining economic success in troubled times (as Henry Ford noted, "the Jew is supremely gifted for business"[26]), and animosity toward them was easy to stir in Hitler's Germany— and it cost millions their lives.

ANTI-SEMITIC PROGRESSION

Persecution of the Jews was carried out in a number of stages. It began well before World War II, with legislation that systematically removed them from society. Following Hitler's takeover of power on January 30, 1933, he began his first nationwide anti-Jewish boycott. Nazis stood outside Jewish businesses throughout Germany to intimidate Jews. The boycott wasn't particularly successful. It was declared that it had served its purpose and was ended after one day.

As chancellor, Hitler finally had the opportunity to legally enforce his ideology, and the Nazi government began enacting legislation to limit the civil and human rights provided to Jews. Following are some the key anti-Semitic laws that paved the way to the Holocaust.

April 7, 1933—Jews are denied the right to hold public office or civil service positions.

April 7, 1933—Jews are no longer allowed to be admitted to the bar to serve in the legal field.

April 25, 1933—The number of Jewish students in public schools is restricted through the Law against Overcrowding in Schools and Universities.

July 14, 1933—The De-Naturalization Law allows the Third Reich to remove the citizenship of Jews and other "undesirables."

October 4, 1933—Jews are denied employment in the press and media.

May 21, 1935—Jews are expelled from the Army.

September 15, 1935—The Nuremberg Laws on Citizenship and Race are introduced, restricting German citizenship to those of German blood. Denied citizenship, Jews lose the right to vote. To protect the "purity of the German blood," marriages between Jews and German citizens are prohibited.

October 15, 1936—By order of the Reich Ministry of Education, Jews are no longer allowed to teach in public schools.

April 9, 1937—By order of the Mayor of Berlin, public schools are not to admit Jewish children until further notice.

March 18, 1938—Jews are no longer allowed to serve as gun merchants.

April 26, 1938—All Jews are forced to report property and assets in excess of 5,000 reichsmarks.

August 17, 1938—Jews are forced to adopt an additional name: "Sara" for women and "Israel" for men.

October 3, 1938—Jewish assets are transferred from Jews to non-Jews.

October 5, 1938—All Jewish passports are considered void unless stamped with the letter "J."

November 12, 1938—All Jewish-owned businesses are closed.

November 15, 1938—All Jewish children are forced out of public schools.

November 28, 1938—To further keep tabs on the location of the Jews, the Reich Ministry of Interior restricts their freedom of movement.

In November 1938, Heinrich Himmler, head of the SS, said, "We must be clear that in the next ten years we will certainly encounter unheard-of critical conflicts. It is not only the struggle of the nations, which in this case are put forward by the opposing side merely as a front, but it is the ideological struggle of the entire Jewry, freemasonry, Marxism, and churches of the world. These forces—of which I presume the Jews to be the driving spirit, the origin of all the negatives—are clear that if Germany and Italy are not annihilated, they will be annihilated. That is a simple conclusion. In Germany the

Jew cannot hold out. This is a question of years. We will drive them out more and more with an unprecedented ruthlessness..."[27]

The message was explicit: anyone or any philosophy that opposed the Nazi agenda would be eliminated. And to the Third Reich, the Jews needed to be the first to go.

Shortly after Himmler's speech came the first physical violence against the Jews on Kristallnacht (Crystal Night), which cemented that such savagery was government endorsed. Herschel Grynszpan, a seventeen-year-old Jewish boy angry that his parents were being deported, shot Ernst vom Rath, a German Third Legation Secretary. Vom Rath died two days later on November 9, 1938, the fifteenth anniversary of the Beer Hall Putsch. It was too ideal of a propaganda opportunity for the Nazis to ignore, and they unleashed violence on a massive scale. On Crystal Night—named for the glass windows that were shattered—over 250 synagogues were demolished, 7,500 Jewish-owned shops vandalized, and over 100 Jews murdered. Some 30,000 Jews were arrested. The massacre furthered anti-Jewish strategy, and, in many Third Reich leaders' minds, permanently linked the ideas of war, expansion, and the need for the elimination of subordinate races. Nearly 80,000

Jews fled Germany after the pogrom.

But Hitler knew that pogroms such as the Crystal Night would not be the ultimate force needed to eliminate the Jews. On January 24, 1939, the Central Office for Jewish Emigration was established, conveying all responsibility to the Nazi SS, and using all possible means to encourage Jews to emigrate.

While Hitler wouldn't reveal his plan for extermination of the Jews to his inner circle until 1941, his rhetoric expanded from the reserved to the implied. On January 30, 1939, he spoke to the Reichstag saying:

> I have very often in my lifetime been a prophet and was mostly derided. In the time of my struggle for power it was in the first instance the Jewish people who received only with laughter my prophecies that I would some time take over the leadership of the state and of the entire people in Germany and then, among other things, also bring the Jewish problem to its solution. I believe that this once hollow laughter of Jewry in Germany has meanwhile already stuck in the throat. I want today to be a prophet again: if international finance Jewry inside and outside Europe should succeed in plunging the nations once more into a world war, the result will be not the bolshevization of the earth and thereby the victory of Jewry, but the annihilation of the Jewish race in Europe![28]

THE HOLOCAUST

The acts of terror and prejudice culminated, as we all know, in the Holocaust. Holocaust is a term based on a Greek word referring to an offering that is "wholly burnt." In the case of Germany and the Nazi regime, it came to mean the government-sanctioned slaughter of more than six million Jews, along with other groups targeted for their supposed racial inferiority and opposing political views. Other victims included gypsies (200,000 murdered), Poles, Soviets (2–3 million prisoners of war were murdered), the mentally and physically disabled (200,000 murdered), communists, socialists, Jehovah's Witnesses, etc.

The Holocaust was a byproduct of the "final solution to the Jewish question"—Hitler's plan to finally eliminate the Jewish population. Prior to the Nazis' rise to power, there were over nine million Jews across Europe. The Holocaust against them began with phases of persecution, segregation, and more severe discriminatory measures, and developed into economic embargos and state-sanctioned violence. The assault on their lives wouldn't come to an end until 1945, and by then, two-thirds of the Jewish population had been eliminated.

With the start of World War II, the Nazis established ghettos and forced labor camps, where the prisoners were literally worked to death, used as slave labor until they died of disease or exhaustion, .

By 1941, mobile killing squads were in full force and as the Third Reich advanced into other countries of Eastern Europe, they murdered over a million Jews and other political opponents. Mobile gas vans were created to accompany the shooting squads. Similar to the eventual gas chambers, these vans came equipped to send deadly amounts of carbon monoxide into enclosed quarters, taking the lives of anyone inside.

In July of that year, Hermann Goering propelled the elimination vision further by beginning implementation of what was referred to as a Final Solution for eliminating the Jews. Fall of 1941 saw Operation Reinhard and the opening of three killing centers in Poland. Others would follow. Ultimately the killing centers would be responsible for taking the lives of 2,700,000 Jews.

On September 29–30, 1941, in a ravine outside Kiev, 33,771 Jews were killed in a single operation. The large crowd was gathered by the local cemetery, expecting to be loaded onto trains. Suddenly they heard machine-gun fire. There was no chance to escape. They were all herded down a corridor of sol-

diers, in groups of ten, and then shot. A truck driver
described the scene:

> One after the other, they had to remove their
> luggage, then their coats, shoes, and over-gar-
> ments and also underwear...Once undressed,
> they were led into the ravine which was about
> 150 meters long and 30 meters wide and a good
> 15 meters deep...When they reached the bottom
> of the ravine they were seized by members of
> the Schutzpolizei and made to lie down on top of
> Jews who had already been shot...The corpses
> were literally in layers. A police marksman came
> along and shot each Jew in the neck with a sub-
> machine gun...I saw these marksmen stand on
> layers of corpses and shoot one after the other...
> The marksman would walk across the bodies
> of the executed Jews to the next Jew, who had
> meanwhile lain down, and shoot him.[29]

Another Jewish prisoner who survived the camp
testified after the war:

> At the extermination camps that had gas cham-
> bers all the prisoners arrived by freight trains.
> At times all the passengers were sent directly
> to gas chambers, but more than often the camp
> doctor inspected them and some were deemed fit
> enough to work in the slave labor camps. The rest
> were moved from the train station platforms to
> an area where they were striped of their clothes
> and possessions. These were seized by the Nazis

to continue to assist is funding the war. Then they were herded naked into the gas chambers, usually being told that they were about to be showered or deloused. There were even signs outside that hung outside saying "baths" and "sauna." To keep them from panicking and causing problems they were sometimes issued with a small piece of soap and a towel, and told to remember where they had left their belongings. When they pleaded for water after their long journey in the cattle trains, they were informed to move along quickly because there was a cup of coffee waiting for them in the camp, and it was getting cold.[30]

Once the chamber was full, the doors were locked and pellets of Zyklon-B were dropped into the chambers through vents, releasing toxic HCN, or hydrogen cyanide. Those inside typically died within twenty minutes, depending on how close they were to a gas vent; about one-third died immediately. Johann Kremer, an SS doctor who oversaw the gassings, testified, "Shouting and screaming of the victims could be heard through the opening and it was clear that they fought for their lives." When the chamber doors were opened, the victims were often found half-squatting, their skin discolored and covered with red and green spots, some foaming at the mouth or bleeding from the ears.[31]

After the gas was pumped out and the dead

bodies removed (which could take up to four hours), gold fillings were pulled from the teeth with pliers by prisoners who were dentists, and the hair was cut from the heads of the women.

The floors and walls of the chamber were then cleaned by Jews who hoped to buy a few extra months of life. When these prisoners had dealt with the dead bodies, the SS conducted a close inspection to ensure that all gold had been removed from the teeth of the corpses. If inspectors found that any gold had been missed, the prisoner responsible was thrown into the furnace alive as punishment.

German physicians carried out cruel experiments on those held in many concentration camps. One of those doctors was the infamous Josef Mengele who worked in Auschwitz. His experiments included putting victims in pressure chambers, testing drugs on them, freezing them, attempting to change their eye colors by injecting chemicals, and various amputations and other brutal surgeries. Those who managed to survive his horrific experiments were almost always killed and dissected shortly afterward.

Mengele liked to experiment with Gypsy children in particular. Vera Alexander was a Jewish inmate at Auschwitz who looked after fifty sets of Romani twins. She recalls, "I remember one set of twins in particular: Guido and Ina, aged about four. One day, Mengele took them away. When they returned, they were in a terrible state: they had been sewn together, back to back, like Siamese twins. Their wounds were infected and oozing pus. They screamed day and night. Then their parents—I remember the mother's name was Stella—managed to get some morphine, and they killed their children in order to end their suffering."[32]

At the Auschwitz concentration camp, where Lieutenant Colonel Rudolf Höss was the first commandant, it is estimated that more than a million people were cruelly murdered.

When the war was coming to a close and Hitler realized the impending defeat, the remaining Jewish prisoners were sent on death marches to prevent their liberation. They would not be free until May 7, 1945, on Victory Day when the Axis powers finally surrendered.

Almost every part of Germany's bureaucracy had a hand in the killing process. Churches and the Interior Ministry produced necessary birth records identifying those who were Jewish. The Finance Ministry confiscated Jewish wealth and property. The Postal Service delivered the notices of deportation and denaturalization. The Transportation department arranged for trains to transfer Jews to concentration camps. Even the private sector cooperated in the efforts. Businesses fired Jewish workers. Pharmaceutical firms tested drugs on camp prisoners. Companies bid for the contracts to build the crematoria. Universities fired Jewish professors and expelled Jewish students. It seems that the whole country unified to make the procedure work like a well-oiled machine.

HITLER,
A CHRISTIAN?

"I may be no pious churchgoer, but deep within me
I am nevertheless a devout man. That is to say,
I believe that he who fights valiantly obeying the
laws which a god has established and who never
capitulates but instead gathers his forces time after
time and always pushes forward—such a man will
not be abandoned by the Lawgiver. Rather, he will
ultimately receive the blessing of Providence."

~ *Adolf Hitler*

*T*HE GREAT CONTRADICTION of Hitler
has always been his theology. Throughout
the rise of the Third Reich, the dissolution
of a democracy, and his construction of the concentration camps, Hitler did a remarkable thing: He
proclaimed a belief in God. How could the man who

said, "I want to raise a generation of young people devoid of a conscience—imperious, relentless, and cruel," possibly have a genuine, sustaining belief in the Almighty?

Moreover, how could a country where 95 percent of the citizens claim affiliation with a Catholic or Protestant church find themselves under the influence of a man who promoted torture, genocide, hatred, and acts of unthinkable brutality? Hitler was a Gatlin gun of spirituality, spraying people with his own manipulative brand of religion, and they bought it. There has to be something in the historical fiber to shed light on this mass seduction of the German church that would inevitably hang swastika banners in its places of worship and allow its leaders to stand side by side, giving a Nazi salute.

In short, Hitler's abuse of theology dismantled the moral fiber of a nation. It created passive onlookers of moral activists. It is unfortunate genius that Hitler could hoodwink a people into believing the Nazi mission was a godly mission. But, as other dictators have done, Hitler captured the power of the church and perverted it for his own use. He became so steeped in his own lies that words of blasphemy began to look—to himself and to others—like words of divine truth.

"What we have to fight for," he wrote in *Mein Kampf*, "is the necessary security for the existence and increase of our race and people, the subsistence of its children and the maintenance of our racial stock unmixed, the freedom and independence of the Fatherland; so that our people may be enabled to fulfill the mission assigned to it by the Creator."[1]

Ultimately, to understand Hitler's abuse of theology is to understand how the Third Reich and its leader were able to prosper. Throughout this chapter we'll take a more in-depth look at a number of crucial issues that contributed to Nazism as a religion and Hitler as its deity.

Was he or wasn't he?

One of the largest questions regarding Hitler is: Was he an atheist or a Christian? Throughout history, both sides have stood their grounds, flinging Hitler to the other opponent, unwilling to claim him as their own. And while I can't blame them for not wanting ownership, the truth is that there's a seemingly reasonable argument that can be made for both sides.

On one hand, looking at the cadre of Hitler's influences, it's no wonder the word "atheist" was thrown around him religiously. He was influenced heavily by Nietzsche, Wagner, and a host of others who had little use for God or Christianity. He showed nothing but a track record of disregard for the commandments of God and was a villain in the most sincere form of the term. His cruelty knew no bounds, believing his critics and dissenters should be "hung on a meat hook and slowly strangled to death with piano wire, the pressure being periodically released to intensify the death agonies."[2] By his hands, a genocide of unthinkable proportions swept across Europe.

On the other hand, however, we have his professions. He claimed a belief in God and said that he was doing God's work. By his own account, Hitler believed that eliminating the Jews was divinely mandated. "Hence today I believe I am acting in accordance with the will of the Almighty Creator," he wrote in *Mein Kampf*. "By defending myself against the Jew, I am fighting for the work of the Lord."

In a speech delivered April 12, 1922, on his way to becoming chancellor, Hitler said:

> For as a Christian I have also a duty to my own people. And when I look on my people I see them work and work and toil and labor, and at the end of the week they have only for their wages wretchedness and misery. When I go out in the morning and see these men standing in their queues and look into their pinched faces, then I believe I would be no Christian, but a very devil, if I felt no pity for them, if I did not, as did our

Lord two thousand years ago, turn against those
by whom today this poor people are plundered
and exploited.[3]

Those who are quick to say that Adolf Hitler was
a Christian are perhaps forgetting a rule of thumb in
much of history: if a politician wants votes he must
profess some sort of faith in God. Then, once in power,
he is free to fulfill his own agenda. If Hitler was anything, he was a master of propaganda. In order for
the Nazi Party to rise, he campaigned for the end of
Marxism to achieve the beginning of peace. In the
people's eye, Hitler was crafted into a figure who
sought morality and unified seemingly irreconcilable
sides. He revived an economy that had been peril-
ously unstable. He shunned the Treaty of Versailles
and built Germany up once again as a military and
world power. He invested in the rebuilding of German
lives and, it appeared, German happiness—putting
crime under his thumb, establishing training schools
for education, but, most important, reinvigorating
a sense of natural pride. People who felt as though
democracy had failed them felt secure in socialism
and had reason for hope in Hitler's leadership.

With the vast majority of the country professing
to be Christian, Hitler needed the continued coop-

eration of the religious communities to achieve his goals. On principle, Hitler needed God so he could claim that his mission and position were divined. It would have been unwise—and in fact impossible—to eradicate the church altogether. What Hitler needed to do instead was alter perceptions, unifying the church under a Nazi mission while recreating the expectations of God. In other words, he had to create another savior.

In terms of religion, he only had to determine what people needed and expected out of their church and then act accordingly to bring all houses under the Nazi agenda.

A NATIONAL CHURCH

Two-thirds of the population held to Protestant Christianity, while one-third was Roman Catholic and a small minority held other beliefs. With the Catholics having a single source of authority in the Vatican, Hitler believed they would be easier to control. In an appeal for Catholic support, he waged a campaign against the "godless movement"[4] to eradicate their common enemies of atheism and communism. By appearing to share their goals, and as a Catholic himself, he convinced the pope to sign a Nazi-Vatican

Concordat (agreement) on July 20, 1933. Promising a peaceful coexistence, the agreement granted the church religious freedom to operate in exchange for their pledge to withdraw from politics and exhibit loyalty to the Reich government. They also pledged that "Catholic religious instruction would emphasize the patriotic duties of the Christian citizen,"[5] which they were more than happy to do.

The Protestants, however, were fractured into over two dozen organizations often reporting to authorities outside of Germany, so Hitler attempted to consolidate them into one national entity that he could easily control. Toward that end, in 1932, Nazi sympathizers formed the "German Christian" movement, but there was little that was "Christian" about this group. It was merely a front for the Nazis to gain political strength through the massive Lutheran church. To join all Protestants into a single, unified body, the Reichstag officially approved the creation of a National Reich Church in July 1933. Hitler applied the pressure to get his devoted follower Ludwig Mueller appointed as head of the newly formed church, with the hope that he would be key in swaying other church leadership to join the national church. The Nazis intimidated anyone who opposed their nominee, and by the time voting day came the

Lutheran candidate had withdrawn and the only choice was: "Do you agree with the Führer that Mueller must be Reich Bishop: Yes or No?"

With Mueller as head of the church, the Nazis then had the power to appoint other leaders. This new Protestant "people's church" gained six hundred thousand followers by the mid-1930s, but that's about the highest it could climb on the charts. Rather than pursue traditional Christian worship, the church used religious rituals as a way to glorify the Nazis and Hitler. Hitler's vision for Germany was clearly laid out in a thirty-point program for the National Reich Church,[6] which should leave no doubt about whether this was truly a Christian endeavor:

THIRTY-POINT PROGRAM FOR THE NATIONAL REICH CHURCH

1. The National Reich's Church of Germany categorically claims the exclusive right and the exclusive power to control all churches within the borders of the Reich; it declares these to be national churches.

2. The German people must not serve the National Reich Church. The National Reich Church is absolutely and exclusively in the service of but one doctrine: race and nation.

3. The field of activity of the National Reich Church will expand to the limits of Germany's territorial and colonial possessions.

4. The National Reich Church does not force any German to seek membership therein. The Church will do everything within its power to secure the adherence of every German soul. Other churches or similar communities and unions particularly such as are under international control or management cannot and shall not be tolerated in Germany.

5. The National Reich Church is determined to exterminate irrevocably and by every means the strange and foreign Christian faiths imported into Germany in the ill-omened year 800.

6. The existing churches may not be architecturally altered, as they represent the property of the German nation, German culture and to a certain extent the historical development of the nation. As property of the German nation, they are not only to be valued but to be preserved.

7. The National Reich Church has no scribes, pastors, chaplains or priests but National Reich orators are to speak in them.

8. National Reich Church services are held only in the evening and not in the morning. These services are to take place on Saturdays with solemn illumination.

9. In the National Reich Church German men and women, German youths and girls will acknowledge God and his eternal works.

10. The National Reich Church irrevocably strives for complete union with the state. It must obey the state as one of its servants. As such, it demands that all landed possessions of all churches and religious denominations be handed over to the state. It forbids that in the future churches should secure ownership of even the smallest piece of German soil or that such be ever given back to them. Not the churches conquer and cultivate land and soil but exclusively the German nation, the German state.

11. National Reich Church orators may never be those who today emphasize with all tricks and cunning verbally and in writing the necessity of maintaining and teaching of Christianity in Germany; they not only lie to themselves but also the German nation, goaded by their love of the positions they hold and the sweet bread they eat.

12. National Reich Church orators hold office, government officials under Civil Service rules.

13. The National Reich Church demands immediate cessation of the publishing and dissemination of the Bible in Germany as well as the publication of Sunday papers, pamphlets, publications and books of a religious nature.

14. The National Reich Church has to take severe measures in order to prevent the Bible and other Christian publications being imported into Germany.

15. The National Reich Church declares that to it, and therefore to the German nation, it has been decided that the Führer's *Mein Kampf* is the greatest of all documents. It is conscious that this book contains and embodies the purest and truest ethics for the present and future life of our nation.

16. The National Reich Church has made it its sacred duty to use all its energy to popularize the coeternal *Mein Kampf* and to let every German live and complete his life according to this book.

17. The National Reich Church demands that further editions of this book, whatever form they may take, be in content and pagination exactly similar to the present popular edition.

18. The National Reich Church will clear away from its altars all crucifixes, Bibles and pictures of Saints.

19. On the altars there must be nothing but *Mein Kampf*, which is to the German nation and therefore to God the most sacred book, and to the left of the altar a sword.

20. The National Reich Church speakers must during church services propound this book to the congregation to the best of their knowledge and ability.

21. The National Reich Church does not acknowledge forgiveness of sins. It represents the standpoint which it will always proclaim that a sin once committed will be ruthlessly punished by the honorable and indestructible laws of nature and punishment will follow during the sinner's lifetime.

22. The National Reich Church repudiates the christening of German children, particularly the christening with water and the Holy Ghost.

23. The parents of a child (or if a newborn child) must only take the German oath before the altar which is worded as follows: The man: "In the name of God I take this Holy oath that I the father of this child, and my wife, are of proven Aryan descent. As a father, I agree to bring up this child in the German spirit and as a member of the German race." The woman: "In the name of God I take this Holy oath that I (name) bore my husband a child and that I its mother am of proven Aryan descent. As a mother, I swear to bring up this child in the German spirit and as a member of the German race." The German diploma can only be issued to newly born children on the strength of the German oath.

24. The National Reich Church abolishes confirmation and religious education as well as the communion the religious preparation for the communion. The educational institutions are and remain the family, the schools, the German youth, the Hitler youth, and the Union of German girls.

25. In order that school graduation of our German youth be given an especially solemn character, all churches must put themselves at the disposal of German youth, the Hitler youth and the Union of German girls on the day of the state's youth which will be on the Friday before Easter. On this day the leaders of these organizations exclusively may speak.

26. The marriage ceremony of German men and women will consist of taking an oath of faithfulness and placing the right hand on the sword. There will not be any unworthy kneeling in National Reich Church ceremonies.

27. The National Reich Church declares the tenth day before Whit Sunday to be the national holiday of the German family.

28. The National Reich Church rejects the customary day of prayer and atonement. It demands that this be transferred to the holiday commemorating the laying of the foundation stone of the National Reich Church.

29. The National Reich Church will not tolerate the establishment of any new clerical religious insignia.

30. On the day of its foundation, the Christian cross must be removed from all churches, cathedrals and chapels within the Reich and its colonies and it must be superseded by the only unconquerable symbol of Germany, the Hakenkreuz [swastika].

As we can see, once Hitler gained power, he attempted to take over the church as he did the nation, effectively removing any Christian influence and making the congregations official vehicles of Nazi propaganda. Any teaching of the Bible was squelched, replaced with reading from *Mein Kampf*; crosses on the altars were exchanged for pictures of Hitler, and Swastika flags were flown above church roofs.

The "German Christian" pastors preached that any teaching about the existence of "sin" was false and had created a complex of weakness in the German people. Biblical Christianity held them back from fulfilling their true destiny, they said, claiming that the German race was divine and that God had chosen a new anointed leader: the blessed Hitler. He was the savior who had been "lifted up" and "would draw all men to himself." He would bring Germany into a new glory—a thousand-year reign.

With the Nazis' political agenda cloaked in biblical phraseology, over time many of the simpler folks were unable to distinguish the true from the false. The Nazi pastors proclaimed that the Old Testament's teachings had allowed the unclean doctrines of the Jew to dominate German thinking. In November 1933, at a massive rally of the "German Christians" in Berlin, they proposed abandoning the Old Testament "with its tales of cattle merchants and pimps" and revising the New Testament with the teaching of Jesus "corresponding entirely with the demands of National Socialism." They drew up resolutions demanding "One People, One Reich, One Faith," requiring all pastors to take an oath of allegiance to Hitler and insisting that all churches include only Aryans and exclude converted Jews.[7]

In a speech at Koblenz on August 26, 1934, Hitler argued for all Christians to unite behind the Reich's vision:

> National Socialism neither opposes the Church nor is it anti-religious, but on the contrary it stands on the ground of a real Christianity. The Church's interests cannot fail to coincide with ours alike in our fight against the symptoms of

> degeneracy in the world of today, in our fight
> against the Bolshevist culture, against an athe-
> istic movement, against criminality, and in our
> struggle for a consciousness of a community in
> our national life...These are not anti-Christian,
> these are Christian principles.[8]

Nonetheless, the Reich Church failed to attract evangelicals to a unified church or to "Nazify" the Protestant congregations. Organized opposition began to arise in 1934, led by Pastor Martin Niemoller and others in what they called the "Confessing Church," which defied Hitler in declaring that it alone was the true, legitimate Protestant church in Germany.

Faced with this open rebellion, the Führer began to take the gloves off. Hitler, the same man who proclaimed his acts were ordained by God, is said to have stated, "I'll make these damn-d parsons feel the power of the state in a way they would have never believed possible. For the moment, I am just keeping my eye upon them: if I ever have the slightest sus-picion that they are getting dangerous, I will shoot the lot of them. This filthy reptile raises its head whenever there is a sign of weakness in the State, and therefore it must be stamped on. We have no sort of use for a fairy story invented by the Jews." [9]

From that point on it was clear: those who didn't

fall in line with Nazism as their guiding religious light would be handled with force. Seven hundred pastors who protested were either murdered and their churches closed, or they quietly disappeared into concentration camps. They were then replaced by Nazi "pastors." As those in the "Confessing Church" continued to protest the Third Reich's anti-Semitism and anti-Christian policies, hundreds of additional pastors would be arrested and their property confiscated. Very few religious leaders had the backbone to challenge the state—the exceptions were figures like the ever admirable Dietrich Bonhoeffer. It wouldn't be until 1937 under Pope Pius XI that Nazi policy would be spoken out against by the Catholic church.

Throughout Germany, the Nazi "pastors" indoctrinated German youth in pulpits and in schools with teachings about their superior "Aryan blood." They taught that Jesus was not a Jew at all, but an Aryan, and that He was a warrior and a hero who died in the fight against Judaism. In twisting Scripture, they claimed that Jesus Himself called the entire Jewish race "children of the devil," and thus began the terrible purging of the Jews from Germany. They mocked the Bible, instructing youth not to worship God but to worship the state and Adolf Hitler as its head. Their one aim was to destroy what they referred to as their "last enemy"—Christianity.

The destruction of Christianity had actually been Hitler's goal even before he took office. Much of the crimes against humanity committed by the Nazi regime were recorded during the Nuremberg war crimes trials of 1945 and 1946. Gen. William J. Donovan of the OSS collected and catalogued the evidence in 148 bound volumes. The publication was called *The Nazi Master Plan: The Persecution of the Christian Churches*, and it summarized Hitler's scheme to undermine and destroy German Christianity, which he called "an integral part of the National Socialist scheme of world conquest."[10]

A number of Nazi leaders have been recorded over the years agreeing that Hitler was far from a Christian; indeed, he was Christianity's worst enemy. Baldur von Schirach, the leader of Hitler Youth, said, "The destruction of Christianity was explicitly recognized as a purpose of the National Socialist movement."[11]

Joseph Goebbels, Hitler's minister of propaganda, noted in his diary in 1939: "The Fuehrer is deeply religious, but deeply anti-Christian. He regards Christianity as a symptom of decay. Rightly so. It is a branch of the Jewish race."[12] In 1939, Hitler even had a Nazi Bible created, which condemned the Jews, removed all non-Aryan passages, and replaced the Ten Commandments with Twelve of his own.

In his memoirs, Albert Speer, the Minister of Armaments and War production for the Third Reich, recorded Hitler's remarks: "You see, it's been our misfortune to have the wrong religion. Why didn't we have the religion of the Japanese, who regard sacrifice for the Fatherland as the highest good? The Mohammedan religion too would have been much more compatible to us than Christianity. Why did it have to be Christianity with its meekness and flabbiness?"[13]

Even the influential German author and historian Konrad Heiden quoted Hitler as saying, "We do not want any other god than Germany itself. It is essential to have fanatical faith and hope and love in and for Germany."[14]

According to William Shirer, who chronicled the Third Reich, "under the leadership of Rosenberg, Bormann, and Himmler, who were backed by Hitler, the Nazi regime intended eventually to destroy Christianity in Germany, if it could."[15]

Still, as a whole, Germans in the 1930s remained hypnotized by Hitler's success in creating jobs, fixing the economy, and restoring Germany's military might. Author William Shirer, who was in Germany during these critical years, sums up the mood of the citizens during this time: "Not many Germans lost sleep over the arrests of a few thousand pastors and priests or over the quarreling of the various Protestant sects..."[16]

WHAT IS A TRUE CHRISTIAN?

As we wonder how Hitler could have claimed to be a Christian, and how the church in Germany could have been duped by his policies, it makes no sense... until we understand something extremely important.

In pre-Second World War Germany, there were 40 million Lutherans. It is significant to realize that to be part of the Lutheran church in those days one need not be converted to Christ. As with the Roman Catholic church, children were simply baptized into the church as infants because they had to be a member to be married or buried. That was just the way it was. If for some reason an individual wanted to separate himself from the church, his name would be read from the pulpit for three Sundays and intercession was then made for him in public prayer. Consequently few took the radical step of leaving the church.

For years the denomination had been influenced by a theological liberalism that was really only secular philosophy disguised by religious language. So rather than being a vibrant Christ-centered lighthouse of biblical truth, the Lutheran church of that time (as with many contemporary denominations) was simply a huge traditional institution. The problem with the German people was that they couldn't recognize true Christianity from hollow religious jargon.

The key to understanding the confusion of Nazi Germany is to understand the biblical concept of true and false believers. Jesus warned that within the church there would be "goats" alongside the "sheep." The true church isn't a building in which Christians meet, neither is it some sectarian group or sect. The true church is an organic thing, a group of believers who make up the Body of Christ. The Body of Christ consists of all genuine believers (those who love God) throughout history, irrespective of denomination or time or location. In reference to true and false believers, the Bible says, "Nevertheless the solid foundation of God stands, having this seal: 'The Lord knows those who are His,' and, 'Let everyone who names the name of Christ depart from iniquity'" (2 Timothy 2:19).

We may be confused about who the goats are and who the sheep are, but God isn't. He knows those who are His, and those who are His have departed from iniquity (sin). Therefore if we don't know Scripture and understand the principles of true and false believers, we are easily confused. We must never forget that Hitler was a dynamic speaker who knew how to use the Christian vernacular. He was able to pull the wool over the eyes of millions of people who were devastated by the collapsed German economy and who were looking for someone to save them from despair. But he was a wolf in sheep's clothing.

Even if one has the credentials of the highest church leader, but is not born again, he cannot rightly claim to be a Christian. The following letter, from pastor and Bible teacher M. Bruce Garner, explains this concept:

> I've lived most of my life in Mexico, and love it so much that in elementary school I spoke, joked and even dreamed in Spanish. Along with learning Spanish, of course, I learned a great deal about Catholicism. Practically all of my classmates were sincere, believing Catholics, and they thought it was a little strange that I was not. As we grew older, I noticed two common reactions from them as they grappled with their faith. Some became disenchanted and dropped out of church completely, doing only what they felt they had to do socially. Others were trying hard to do everything Catholicism had taught them they must do to someday be in heaven. They went to Catechism, attended Mass, and even went regularly to confession.

But according to the Bible, my friends and I were all in the same sort of trouble: none of us could be accepted on our own merits by a perfectly holy and righteous God. Not a single one of us could ever be declared righteous by God because we had kept all of His Commandments. On the contrary, we had broken them! There was no real difference between us. What we needed was a Savior. We didn't need to try harder—we'd still fall short of God's standard. We already had. We always would.

This came as a shock to my friends who took the time to humbly consider it. Their own Bibles, beginning with the Ten Commandments, showed them how far they had fallen short of God's standard. When they stopped comparing themselves with one another ("Well, at least I'm not as bad as that guy!") and considered what God, the Lawgiver and Judge, would say about them, they realized their need.

They were close to the truth. They had been told that God loved them. (And He does!) They knew that Jesus had died on the cross in payment for their sin, and many of them had crucifixes over their beds and on chains around their necks that reminded them of His sacrifice. But even then, knowing and believing all this, they were in deadly danger. They had been busy with religious activity, but they had not measured themselves by God's standard—His moral Law.

God's standard, not religion, showed them they had lied, committed adultery (at least in their heart), dishonored their parents, and taken

God's holy name in vain. They had committed, just as I had, a host of offenses against God. It was then that they realized that their best efforts to earn their own salvation were in vain.

It is the Law that shows us that our "good works" will never be sufficient. It shows us that we're already in danger of judgment, because we've already offended the Judge.

The Law shows us God's awesome holiness. It shows us our utter inability to ever do enough to satisfy His righteous demands. This realization is humbling for everyone. It humbled me, and it humbled some of my friends. But it didn't end our spiritual life—it actually began it! It made us see our need and turn for mercy to Jesus. It was then that we were born again.

At the age of twenty-two, I too was born again, and became a Christian. That experience was evidenced by certain radical life changes. These evidences are what the Bible calls "the things that accompany salvation" (Hebrews 6:9).

As we have seen, Hitler was brought up as a Roman Catholic, but evidence shows that he had never been born again, or become a Christian. This is evident because he didn't exhibit the signs that accompany salvation. Many Protestants and Catholics are in this category.

The Bible makes it clear that someone is not a

Christian until he is born again, and that the new birth must take place for anyone to enter Heaven (see John 3:3,7). Those who are intellectual believers but have never been born again spiritually are not Christians. They may be religious. They may attend church. But it is incorrect to label anyone in such a case a "Christian." This isn't just my opinion, but is from Jesus Himself. He told Nicodemus, a very religious man, "Most assuredly, I say to you, unless one is born again, he cannot see the kingdom of God." When Nicodemus was understandably confused, Jesus said again, "Most assuredly, I say to you, unless one is born of water and the Spirit, he cannot enter the kingdom of God. That which is born of the flesh is flesh, and that which is born of the Spirit is spirit. Do not marvel that I said to you, 'You must be born again'" (John 3:1–7).

There is something that separates Christianity from all the religions of the world. It's the knowledge of the spiritual nature of God's Law. That was what brought me from an intellectual knowledge of God to a point of knowing that I needed to be born again. Those who don't have knowledge of the spiritual nature of the Law can only think of God in terms of human standards. Psalm 50 puts it this way:

> But to the wicked God says: "What right have
> you to declare My statutes, or take My covenant
> in your mouth, seeing you hate instruction and
> cast My words behind you? When you saw a
> thief, you consented with him, and have been a
> partaker with adulterers. You give your mouth
> to evil, and your tongue frames deceit. You sit
> and speak against your brother; you slander
> your own mother's son. These things you have
> done, and I kept silent; you thought that I was
> altogether like you." (Psalm 50:16–21)

Notice the references to the Seventh, Eighth, and
Ninth Commandments, prohibiting adultery, theft,
and lying. Here is someone who "declares" God's stat-
utes and takes His covenant in their mouth, but they
hate instruction. There are many in that category who
have a measure of spirituality but refuse to heed the
warning that Jesus Himself (the very One they profess to serve) gave about the absolute necessity of the
new birth. Then we see the root of their error: they
thought God was just like them. They thought God
didn't mind theft and adultery. Yet the Scriptures tell
us that when we as much as look with lust, we commit
adultery in the heart: "You have heard that it was said
to those of old, 'You shall not commit adultery.' But I
say to you that whoever looks at a woman to lust for
her has already committed adultery with her in his

heart" (Matthew 5:27,28).

That's what is known as the spirituality of the Law. In other words, God's Law doesn't simply require an outward appearance of piety or some religious good works. It requires holiness of the thought-life (see Romans 7:14). If we even hate someone, God considers us to be murderers: "Whoever hates his brother is a murderer, and you know that no murderer has eternal life abiding in him" (1 John 3:15).

The Law and God are like the sun and its light. We can never separate the two. The moral Law (the Ten Commandments) is the very essence of His holy character. The Scriptures tell us that both the Law and God are perfect, holy, just, and good. It reveals His likes and dislikes. It is a synopsis of His core attributes. There wasn't a time in eternity when God said, "I wonder what is right and wrong." The Law is eternal, and it's universal—it is applicable to the entire human race.

Perhaps that fact is why Hitler hated God's Law and sought to eradicate the Ten Commandments:

> The day will come when I shall hold up against these commandments the tables of a new law. And history will recognize our movement as the great battle for humanity's liberation, a liberation from the curse of Mount Sinai, from

the dark stammerings of nomads who could no more trust their own sound instincts, who could understand the divine only in the form of a tyrant who orders one to do the very things one doesn't like. This is what we are fighting against: the masochistic spirit of self-torment, the curse of so-called morals, idolized to protect the weak from the strong in the face of immortal law of battle, the great law of divine nature. Against the so-called Ten Commandments, against them we are fighting.[17]

God not only gave Israel the moral Law, writing the Ten Commandments on stone so that they would know His will, He has also written His law upon the heart of each person. His moral code is embedded in the heart of every human being so we know right from wrong.

It was no surprise to humanity that God says it was wrong to kill, lie, steal, blaspheme, covet, dishonor our parents, and commit adultery. The human conscience is in agreement. But the most important commandment is the First. Here it is in context with the Second:

You shall have no other gods before Me.

You shall not make for yourself a carved image—any likeness of anything that is in heaven above, or that is in the earth beneath, or that is in the water under the earth; you shall not bow down to them nor serve them. For I, the Lord your god, am a jealous God, visiting the iniquity of the fathers upon the children to the third and fourth generations of those who hate Me, but showing mercy to thousands, to those who love Me and keep My commandments. (Exodus 20:1–17)

These two Commandments must not be separated. God should be first in our affections, and we fail to put Him first when we make an "image" of what we think He is like. Many other religions think it is okay or even necessary to make an image of their gods. However, we can create an image of God with our hands by carving out our concept of Him in stone or in wood, or we can create an image of what we think He is like in our minds. Either way, when we bow down to our created god we violate both the First and the Second of the Ten Commandments.

It was clear that Hitler believed in God. The important distinction is that Hitler didn't believe in the God revealed in the Bible. It was entirely a god of his own devising. He imagined a god who condones murder, lying, and theft, giving him license to say, "My conduct is in accordance with the will of the Almighty Creator"—when in fact he was clearly going against His will and was guilty of idolatry. Jesus warned His own disciples that the time would come when people would kill them, thinking that they were doing God a favor (see John 16:2). Thus the soil of human history is soaked in the blood of the innocents—the horrific fruit of the sin of idolatry. The church's most staunch opposition has always come from those who create a concept of god in their own minds and then wield a sharp and bloody sword to advance its cause.

The simple truth is: Hitler wasn't a Christian; he was a compulsive liar. He was also a thief who stole millions in goods from the Jews. He was a covetous man who coveted other nations. First John 4:7-8 tells Christians to "love one another, for love is of God; and everyone who loves is born of God and knows God. He who does not love does not know God, for God is love." The hate-filled Hitler didn't love or know God. He was an idolater who created a god in his own image. He was a blasphemer—with his twisted ravings about the purposes and nature of a holy God—and he murdered millions.

At the end of the day, the only evidence of Hitler's Christianity is his own rhetoric. He said he was a follower of Christ, so should we take that at face value? While perhaps it seems silly to say this, maybe we should be wary of taking such a man at his own word. Hitler's greatest strength, and ultimately the main reason he was able to come to power, was due to his proclivity for propaganda and manipulation. Hitler knew he was a leader of a largely Christian nation and that very little can rouse individuals' actions, obedience, and reverence more than religion. So, playing his infamous propaganda card, he saw the inherent value of the church and exploited it.

Ultimately Hitler did far more than capture the power of the church and pervert if for his own use. He went further and preached a perverted understanding of God, for his own use.

MESSIANIC COMPLEX

It is human nature to project your ideas and beliefs onto something or someone else. And it is difficult to be completely objective and not shape things to fit your own ideals. A while back this idea was epitomized in the popular question "What would Jesus do?" To many both inside and of outside the church, "Jesus" became synonymous for the right thing to do. Books hit the market asking what would Jesus eat and what would He drive? The question sounds legitimate, but it is so open-ended. Without being grounded in Scripture, the question alone is open to interpretation. Without proper grounding, we are easily deceived; we even deceive ourselves.

Adolf Hitler not only created his own image of God, he created his own image of Jesus Christ. Jesus can be shaped into any image our fertile imaginations want Him to become. He could be just a great teacher or a great leader. Or He could be merely seen as a great historical figure. This was John Lennon's mistake when he said in an interview, "We're more popular than Jesus."[18] He didn't see Jesus as who He is—the Creator of the universe in human form (see Colossians 1:13–21). Albert Einstein had a wonderful image of Jesus. He said, "No man can deny the fact that Jesus existed, nor that his sayings are beautiful. Even if some of them have been said before, no one has expressed them so divinely as he." Yet there is no record of Einstein calling Jesus "Lord."[19]

As Hitler became consumed with the idea of his own power, he began giving himself God-like status, comparing himself directly with Christ:

> When I came to Berlin a few weeks ago...the luxury, the perversion, the iniquity, the wanton display, and the Jewish materialism disgusted me so thoroughly that I was almost beside myself. I nearly imagined myself to be Jesus Christ when

He came to His Father's temple and found it taken by the money-changers. I can well imagine how He felt when He seized a whip and scourged them out.[20]

Now and then Hitler would refer to himself as "a voice crying in the wilderness," or as John the Baptist who was preparing the way of the Lord, making His path straight, so that He could come and lead Germany to power and glory. The more power Hitler wielded, the more he saw himself as the Messiah. He referenced the Bible and used religious language to describe the movement. He wholeheartedly assumed the godlike role he perpetuated.

"Christ has come to us through Adolf Hitler," declared Pastor Leutheuser, a leader of the "German Christian" movement, on August 30, 1933. "He was the decisive figure when the people were just about to go under. Hitler struck out for us and through his power, his honesty, his faith, and his idealism, the Redeemer found us...We know today the Saviour has come...We have only one task, be German, not be Christian."[21]

And so the religion of Nazism abounded. In Hitler's messianic complex, he saw himself not even as a vehicle for God's work, but actually as God Himself whose divine purpose was to rescue Germany from its clearly deteriorating state. "What Christ began," he said, "I will complete."

In the Hitler Youth, children were taught a salute to Hitler modeled after the Lord's Prayer:

> Adolf Hitler, you are our great Führer. Thy name makes the enemy tremble. Thy Third Reich comes; they will alone is law upon the earth. Let us hear daily thy voice and order us by the leadership, for we will obey to the end and even with our lives. We praise thee! Heil Hitler!
>
> Führer, my Führer, given me by God, protect and preserve my life for long. You saved Germany in time of need. I thank you for my daily bread. Be with me for a long time, do not leave me, Führer, my Führer, my faith, my light, Hail to my Führer![22]

Equally alarming, when Hitler came to power he required members of the armed forces as well as civil servants to swear allegiance not to Germany or to the flag, but to him personally as supreme ruler, through the Führer Oath: "I swear by God this sacred oath, that I will render unconditional obedience to Adolf Hitler, the Führer of the German Reich and people, Supreme Commander of the Armed Forces, and will as a brave soldier be ready to risk my life at any time for this oath."[23]

Hitler trained his disciples well. Each of them parroted his spiritual convictions for the sake of the Reich. Like Hitler, they spoke of the holiness of their work and of Hitler being "sent by God."

"God gave the savior to the German people. We have faith, deep and unshakeable faith," gushed Hermann Goering, "that he [Hitler] was sent to us by God to save Germany."[24]

Joseph Goebbels, Hitler's Propaganda Minister, described the deportation of the Jews to the camps in 1942 by claiming, "A judgment is being carried out on the Jews which is barbaric, but fully deserved."[25] It's clear that Goebbels saw Hitler and the Nazis as the supreme judges over the Jewish people. He spoke of Hitler as "either Christ or St. John."

However, the Bible is not a smorgasbord, where the reader picks and chooses only that which is sweet to his palate. It is an instruction book for sinners. Those who continue to do what is abhorrent to God show themselves to be unregenerate. Though his Roman Catholic parents raised him in that faith, Goebbels was unconverted. Toward the end of the bloody and murderous Nazi rampage, he wrote, "Rarely in history has a brave people struggling for its life faced such terrible tests as the German people have in this war...The misery that results for us all, the never ending chain of sorrows, fears, and spiritual torture does not need to be described in detail We are bearing a heavy fate because we are fighting for a good cause, and are called to bravely endure the battle to achieve greatness."[26]

In his spiritually warped mind, Goebbels believed that the pains of war that Germany was suffering were for the sake of justice. Consider his perversion of the character of Jesus of Nazareth: "Christ is the genius of love, as such the most diametrical opposite of Judaism, which is the incarnation of hate. The Jew is a non-race among the races of the earth...Christ is the first great enemy of the Jews...that is why Judaism had to get rid of him. For he was shaking the very foundations of its future international power. The Jew is the lie personified. When he crucified Christ, he crucified everlasting truth for the first time in history."[27]

Jesus was not "the first great enemy of the Jews," as He Himself was Jewish (see John 4:9; 18:35), as were His mother and Joseph. His disciples were Jewish. The first three thousand Christian converts were Jews. Jesus was sent to the Jewish people by God (see Matthew 15:24) because God loved the Jews with an everlasting love (see Jeremiah 31:2–4).

Even Goebbels's understanding of the crucifixion is unbiblical. The cross was an evident display of God's love for humanity, both Jew and Gentile. Romans 5:8 says that "God demonstrates His own love toward us, in that while we were still sinners, Christ died for us."

In his attempt to win the eternal gratitude of Hitler, Goebbels further wrote, "Christ cannot have been a Jew. I do not need to prove this with science or scholarship. It is so!"[28] To claim that Jesus was not a Jew, Goebbels had to completely disregard the geologies of Jesus Christ recorded in the Gospels. They trace His Jewish lineage through the line of David all the way back to Adam. Goebbels continued to show his ignorance of Jesus in saying, "I believe that the first Christian, Christ himself, would discover more of his teaching in our actions than in this theological hair-splitting."[29] I wonder how after the Holocaust he reconciled the murderous policies of the Third Reich with these words of Jesus:

> "But I say to you who hear: Love your enemies, do good to those who hate you, bless those who curse you, and pray for those who spitefully use you. To him who strikes you on the one cheek, offer the other also. And from him who takes away your cloak, do not withhold your tunic either. Give to everyone who asks of you. And from him who takes away your goods do not ask them back. And just as you want men to do to you, you also

do to them likewise.

"But if you love those who love you, what credit is that to you? For even sinners love those who love them. And if you do good to those who do good to you, what credit is that to you? For even sinners do the same. And if you lend to those from whom you hope to receive back, what credit is that to you? For even sinners lend to sinners to receive as much back. But love your enemies, do good, and lend, hoping for nothing in return; and your reward will be great, and you will be sons of the Most High. For He is kind to the unthankful and evil." (Luke 6:27–35)

Goebbels was clearly guilty of creating "another Jesus." Hitler, his spiritual leader, did the same. According to a 1941 psychological profile, "Hitler has very little admiration for Christ, the Crucified. Although he was brought up a Catholic, and received Communion, during the war, he severed his connection with the Church directly afterwards. This kind of Christ he considers soft and weak and unsuitable as a German Messiah."[30]

Scripture warns about a false gospel and following a false Jesus (2 Corinthians 11:4): "For if he who comes preaches another Jesus whom we have not preached, or if you receive a different spirit which you have not received, or a different gospel which

you have not accepted—you may well put up with it!"
The Nazis certainly preached a different gospel, con-
sisting of another Jesus, and look at the condemnation
the Scriptures pronounce upon those who do such:
"But even if we, or an angel from heaven, preach any
other gospel to you than what we have preached to
you, let him be accursed" (Galatians 1:8).

WHAT ABOUT YOU?

As mentioned previously, it's human tendency to
deceive even ourselves. Perhaps you are a spiritual
person, and you have been living your life doing the
best you can. You believe in God. You do kind things
for others. You confess your sins to God, but you have
never been born again. So please take a moment to
look to the Law and let it examine you. Put yourself
on the stand and let its light reveal what you are
before the Day of Judgment.

Have you ever lied? Have you stolen anything
in your life, regardless of the value? Have you ever
used God's name in vain, even once? Have you ever
looked with lust or hated anyone? If you have done
these things, then you are a self-admitted lying thief,
a blasphemer, a murderer, and an adulterer at heart.
With that assessment, what would you have to say

for yourself before God? How could you honestly justify murder, adultery, lying, stealing, and using God's name as a cuss word? Don't deceive yourself into thinking that simply confessing your sins will help you. That is like standing before a judge and confessing that you are guilty as charged. How could that help? Saying you are sorry and that you won't do it again won't help either. Of course a criminal should be sorry and of course he shouldn't commit the crimes again. So what are you going to say to make things right? How can you avoid the damnation of Hell? This is where the good news comes in. We can't help ourselves. All we can do is raise our hands in surrender.

A Protestant, Catholic, or any religious person who is not born again is almost certainly trusting in their own goodness or their own religious "works" to save them on Judgment Day. They are trusting in their praying, fasting, repentance, their "good" works, etc. However, a Christian is someone who trusts in the person of Jesus Christ alone for his eternal salvation. This is because the Law has shown him that his good works aren't "good." He suddenly understands that in God's eyes he is a criminal, and that God is a perfect Judge. Therefore anything he offers Him isn't good at all, but is actually an attempt to bribe the Judge to dismiss his case.

If we stand in the presence of a holy God, we will get something worse than the death sentence. We will be damned. Fortunately, the Bible tells us that God is "rich in mercy" (see Ephesians 2:4). Jesus told a parable of a loving father who was watching for the return of his prodigal son. Then, when he saw him, he ran to his son, fell upon him and kissed him. You are I are the prodigal, and God is the father. Look at what He did to save guilty sinners from damnation in Hell! God became a human being in Jesus of Nazareth, and the reason He did this was to pay our fine so that we could leave the courtroom. That's what took place on that terrible cross 2,000 years ago. The sin of the world fell upon the innocent Son of God—He was bruised for our iniquities.

Notice the repetition of the words "only begotten" in these verses from God's Word:

> And the Word became flesh and dwelt among us, and we beheld His glory, the glory as of the only begotten of the Father, full of grace and truth...No one has seen God at any time. The only begotten Son, who is in the bosom of the Father, He has declared Him...For God so loved the world that He gave His only begotten Son, that whoever believes in Him should not perish but have everlasting life... He who believes in Him is not condemned; but he who does not believe is condemned already, because he has not believed in the name of the only begotten Son of

God (John 1:14,18, 3:16,18).

The words "only begotten" mean that Jesus was absolutely unique. He was the only One who could pay for the sin of the world because He was morally perfect, and He was morally perfect because He was God in human form. And He proved this not only by suffering for our sins, but by resurrecting Himself from the dead:

> Therefore My Father loves Me, because I lay down My life that I may take it again. No one takes it from Me, but I lay it down of Myself. I have power to lay it down, and I have power to take it again. This command I have received from My Father. (John 10:17,18)

So what are you going to do? Are you going to stay religious, trusting in yourself, or are you going to surrender to the Savior and trust in Him alone? Please surrender. Now. Confess your sins to God and then turn from them. God will help you. And then make sure that your trust is in Jesus Christ alone. Transfer your trust from yourself to the Savior. If you are not sure what to say, pray a prayer similar to the one below. After David committed adultery and murder and his sin was exposed, he cried:

Have mercy upon me, O God, According to Your lovingkindness; According to the multitude of Your tender mercies, Blot out my transgressions. Wash me thoroughly from my iniquity, And cleanse me from my sin. For I acknowledge my transgressions, And my sin is always before me. Against You, You only, have I sinned, And done this evil in Your sight— That You may be found just when You speak, And blameless when You judge. Behold, I was brought forth in iniquity, And in sin my mother conceived me. Behold, You desire truth in the inward parts, And in the hidden part You will make me to know wisdom. Purge me with hyssop, and I shall be clean; Wash me, and I shall be whiter than snow. Make me hear joy and gladness, That the bones You have broken may rejoice. Hide Your face from my sins, And blot out all my iniquities. Create in me a clean heart, O God, And renew a steadfast spirit within me. (Psalm 51:1–10)

· 7 ·

THE HAND OF PROVIDENCE

"Hitler has disgraced Germany for all time! He betrayed and disgraced the people that loved him!...I will be the first to admit my guilt."

~ Hans Frank, the "Jew Butcher of Cracow"

WHEN WE READ about the atrocities of the Nazi regime, it is easy to ask who was in control. Hitler certainly proclaimed that he was divinely led by God and that everything that had and would occur was a result of a great reality called Fate. When he took hold of Vienna, he said to the welcoming crowds that swarmed to his arrival, "I believe that it was God's will to send a youth from here into the Reich, to let him grow up, to raise him to be the leader of the nation so as to enable him to lead his homeland into the Reich. There is a higher ordering...I felt that now the call of Providence had come to me. And that which took place in three days was only conceivable as the fulfillment of the wish and the will of this Providence."[1]

Throughout his rise and reign, Hitler's speeches were laden with heavy doses of "fate" and "providence." But if he was the one who was called and aligning the stars, where had God gone? If God promises to always be with us, why does it seem as though He's absent in our most despairing moments?

Why does God let evil prosper?

I wept a number of times while writing this book. I stared in horror at photos of soldiers shooting Jews. I saw picture after picture of piles of dead, emaciated bodies—women and children starved close to the point of death as an experiment. With my hands cupped over my mouth, I sat transfixed at the sight of the bodies of poor women, hanging by the neck, as Nazi soldiers smiled at their pathetic struggles in death.

Through tear-filled eyes I read testimonies of those who witnessed Jews being shot and buried alive. I sobbed uncontrollably as I saw the picture of a mother who was clutching a toddler in her arms as a soldier shot her in the head. I felt sick with shame that anyone could do such things to other human beings. I wanted to scream with outrage and ask why God hadn't put a stop to this unspeakable horror.

The obvious question is the hardest one. Why does God allow these things to take place? There were times in the Bible when He saw fit to send lightning as punishment. He killed people for lying (Acts 5:1-6), for sexual misconduct (Genesis 38:10), among other things. Do lying and sexual sins provoke divine retribution while the torturous murder of millions is not worthy of intervention? Why didn't God kill Hitler before he exterminated so many innocent people? He opened up the Red Sea and killed the Egyptians when they chased the Jews. The Scriptures tell us that nothing is impossible for God, so why didn't He stop such dreadful evil?

If I have the ability to rescue a family from murder and I fail to intervene, then I'm guilty of what our society's civil law calls "depraved indifference." If I stand by and watch, I would have their blood on my hands. As human beings, we exist with a moral compass. We demand that evil be penalized because we are made in God's image. We want justice because we have an inherent knowledge of right and wrong, and so we are deeply disturbed when true evil goes unpunished. So it's obvious we would struggle with the suffering that was so prevalent in the Holocaust and the perpetrator that seemed to get away so easily. Where was God in Nazi Germany? And where was God in Adolf Hitler?

SURVIVING THE ODDS

Hitler did not have good odds of survival. There were a number of times in his life that his hopes, and even his heartbeat, should have been cut short. Do you recall how many of his siblings died in childbirth or in their childhood years? For some reason he survived when the others did not. Likewise, Hitler served with no reservations in World War I. The majority of his company died, and yet he still persisted in taking risky assignments. His likelihood of survival was minimal, but he made it out of the war more determined in his ideology than ever.

While he was a budding political leader, the prior regimes should have quickly snuffed out his light, but even as a "traitor" he was punished lightly, even treated heroically. They let him off the hook and back into the water. With the failure of the Beer Hall Putsch, Hitler said, "We knew that we were carrying out the will of Providence, and we were being guided by a higher power...Fate meant well with us. It did not permit an action to succeed which, if it had succeeded, would in the end have inevitably crashed as a result of the movement's inner immaturity in those days and its deficient organizational and intellectual foundation." By his own mouth he proclaimed that his past failures would be the gateway to his future success.

Later as Führer, there were a number of assassination attempts on his life—plausible moments for God to step in and bring the murderer to his own demise. On July 20, 1944, during a meeting in Rastenberg, East Prussia, at Hitler's headquarters known as the "Wolf's Lair," Claus Schenk Graf von Stauffenberg, a senior officer in the Nazi regime, placed a briefcase bomb under the table near Hitler. The bomb exploded, but Hitler miraculously survived virtually unscathed, coming away with only a few minor burns and a concussion. That afternoon, he even kept his appointment with Italy's Benito Mussolini. The German news, in a typical display of Hitler propaganda, reported: "The attempt which has failed must be a warning to every German to redouble his war effort," said the newsreader. And the deputy head of press, Helmut Suendermann, stated, "The German people must consider the failure of the attempt on

Hitler's life as a sign that Hitler will complete his tasks under the protection of divine power."[2]

Finally someone had the courage to try to stop this murderous beast and save the precious lives of perhaps millions of people who would die in the final year of the war. And, unbelievably, Hitler survived! The guilty were then rounded up and executed, and Hitler came away emboldened in his evil agenda and, of all things, boasting of divine protection.

Just after being elected in 1933, Hitler remarked, "Who says I am not under the special protection of God?"

It indeed seemed Hitler was under a special protection. But why did God allow him to slip through the cracks? Why does God allow any evil?

BROADEN THE QUESTION

Before we answer this question, let's broaden it a little. The mystery isn't that God just allows evil to exist, but He allows unspeakable suffering. More than sixteen thousand children to die of hunger-related causes each day on God's fair earth.[3] That's one child gasping for its last breath every five seconds. Over one hundred children have died since you started this chapter. All they needed to live was a little food, or some rain to fall from the heavens. God fed Israel with manna from Heaven and quail that fell from the sky. Doesn't the sight of emaciated little children lying in the dirt, with flies crawling across their lifeless eyes, move the heart of a compassionate God?

Is He moved with empathy at the sight of families being horrifically crushed in car accidents, and screaming in agony while waiting to be rescued? I'm sure paramedics have horror stories of people trapped in burning vehicles. More than forty thousand people meet their deaths in car accidents each year, and that's just in the United States.

Then there's the heart-rending sight of kids with cancer. My daughter's friend has a twelve-year-old with cancer. She has been operated on and cut into so many times, she is pleading to die. Her parents are Christians, and their anguish is immeasurable. And that scenario is played out many times daily throughout this sorry old earth.

Add to that the thousands of other terrible diseases that people contract, the murders, the torture, the vicious rapes, and all the other evils that take place every day, and you have a living nightmare.

To answer this important question, let me tell you about my father. He regularly left my mother and us kids. When he was around, there were times when he would physically hit us. I remember him once killing a defenseless animal with his bare hands. With that information, you would be quite justified in concluding that my father was a tyrant—an abusive beast of a man.

But here's some missing information that will radically change your perspective. He regularly left our mother to take care of us because he was a builder, and he worked long hours to make money to buy food for his beloved family. He physically spanked us kids when we lied or stole anything; he cared enough to correct us when we did wrong. Oh, and that helpless animal—he found it on the side of the road. It had been hit by a car and was dying. He put the poor animal out of its misery, and it grieved him to have to do it. My dad was a loving father and an extremely compassionate person.

Many times I have heard angry atheists and bitter skeptics paint God as a tyrant. They accuse Him of being a heartless monster because of his inaction when it comes to suffering and because of some of His actions in the Old Testament. Granted, His judgments throughout the Old Testament are very harsh. But they are also harsh in the New Testament.

But let me give you some information that should radically change your thoughts. God gave us life. He gave us eyes to see this incredible creation. He gave us ears to hear beautiful music. He gave us taste buds to enjoy all the incredible variety of food. Every time we see a breathtaking sunset, or play with a cute puppy, or look into the eyes of a newborn baby, we are looking at His creation.

He has lavished His kindness upon us by giving us all the blessings of this life, and what does sinful humanity do? We use His name as a cuss word. We are unthankful and ungrateful for His kindness and deliberately violate His Law. So what did He do? He became a perfect Man in the person of Jesus of Nazareth. The first time Jesus opened His mouth to preach, his enemies tried to kill Him. Scripture records that sinful man tried to murder Him ten times before they finally succeeded.

This incredibly kind, loving, and forgiving God is also a God of justice and truth. His very nature demands that when a man murders another human being, he must be punished. His righteousness cries out for justice to be done when anyone transgresses His perfect Law. So what did God do further? He gave His life on a cruel cross, taking the punishment for the sin of the world, so that evil humanity could escape just punishment in Hell.

So when I see God's harsh judgments in Scripture or think of His inaction when it comes to evil, I have a counterbalance. I don't see my heavenly Father as a cold and impersonal tyrant, because the Bible gives us extra information—it says that all of His judgments are righteous and true altogether. That terrible cross shows us that His wrath against evil hasn't changed, but it also gives us a glimpse of His incredible love and mercy, goodness and kindness, compassion and care.

So when angry men point their finger at God and accuse Him of evil, I say with the Psalmist, "Righteous are You, O Lord, when I plead with You; Yet let me talk with You about Your judgments. Why does the way of the wicked prosper? Why are those happy who deal so treacherously?" (Jeremiah 12:1). But I ask it in anguish of heart without any hint of accusation. I don't question God's holy character because I fear Him, and as a wise Jew once said, "The fear of the Lord is the beginning of wisdom" (Proverbs 9:10). God always has His reasons. Who am I to stand in moral judgment over Almighty God, especially in the light of my own sinful heart? Such arrogance on my part would indeed be a delusion of grandeur.

The Bible says that we shall all stand before God one day (see Romans 14:12). I am eternally grateful that on that "great and terrible day" my sins are forgiven. I don't have to have my personal Nuremberg trial for my crimes against God. My fine was fully paid two thousand years ago. I will face God, not as my Judge, but as my Savior. And when I see Him face-to-face, He may even condescend to answer my questions. And He may answer yours too...if you have turned from your own sins, and you are trusting in Jesus Christ alone for your salvation. That is my deepest prayer and hope, because it is for you that I wrote this book.

ANOTHER HOLOCAUST

As we consider how God could have allowed the Holocaust in Nazi Germany, I see parallels with another holocaust closer to home. One of the great mysteries about the Holocaust was the seeming complicity of so many of the German people. Yet I have watched World War II footage of the Allies as they liberated concentration camps, forcing those who lived around the death camps to go through them. The civilians walked in with smiles on their faces and came out grief-stricken and horrified. I was left wondering, How could they not know? They lived around the camps and could see the acrid smoke constantly billowing from the chimneys. Didn't they know what was going on in their own backyard? Did they know, but out of fear of the Nazis they remained silent while millions of innocent people were put to death? Or did they seriously think that the camps were nothing more than some sort of wartime confinement housing for Jews?

Do you know about America's holocaust? Do you know about what's going on in your own backyard? Or do you know that millions of innocent unborn babies are being put to death in abortion, but you think that it's not a baby in the womb and therefore it's okay to remain silent? Perhaps you think that whatever it is that's growing within the womb is not human, and therefore can be eliminated like common waste. It's okay to get rid of it because it's not human. That's what Hitler said of the Jews. He declared that they weren't human, so that he could justify their elimination.

Yet, we do know when life begins, and it's not when you or I or the mother feels it begins. According to science, it is at conception:

> "Biologically speaking, human development begins at fertilization."
>
> ~ *The Biology of Prenatal Development, National Geographic, 2006*

"The two cells gradually and gracefully become one. This is the moment of conception, when an individual's unique set of DNA is created, a human signature that never existed before and will never be repeated."

~ In the Womb, National Geographic, 2005

After fertilization has taken place a new human being has come into being. [It] is no longer a matter of taste or opinion...it is plain experimental evidence. Each individual has a very neat beginning, at conception."

~ Dr. Jerome LeJeune, Professor of Genetics, University of Descartes

"By all the criteria of modern molecular biology, life is present from the moment of conception."

~ Professor Hymie Gordon, Mayo Clinic[5]

The American Medical Association (AMA) declared as far back as 1857 (referenced in the Roe. vs. Wade opinion) that "the independent and actual existence of the child before birth, as a living being" is a matter of objective science.

So at the moment of conception there is infant human development. There is a living entity with its own unique DNA. So with those thoughts in mind, help me to finish this sentence if you can: "It's okay to kill a baby in the womb when _____."

Perhaps you answered that a pregnancy could be morally terminated in the case of rape. But why would you kill the child for the crime of the father? Which is worse, rape or murder? Why not support the mother and then have the baby adopted? Isn't it better to have a child adopted rather than kill it? If you don't like the thought of adoption and prefer abortion, could you kill the child yourself by cutting it in pieces, or would that be too difficult so you would rather that a doctor do it for you?

How do you even make a moral decision about an important subject such as abortion? How do you know right from wrong? For example, how do you know if adultery is wrong? How about murder? Theft? Is theft ever right? Not according to the Bible. Even if you steal to feed yourself because you are starving, it is still wrong, and, according to Scripture, if you are caught you have to pay seven times the amount you stole (see Proverbs 6:30–32).

Hopefully you know that murder and adultery are never right. So if you know that both murder and adultery are morally wrong, from where do you get that knowledge? If it is from what society says is right and wrong, you have a problem. Remember, everything that Hitler did was completely legal. In the case of Nazi Germany, society ruled murder to be right, and we live in a society that has done the same with the unborn.

If you and I advocate the taking of a human life in the womb as a "right," then how are we any different from those who advocated the taking of the lives of so many Jews? The answer is that we are not.

If you don't know God, and you become "born again" (see John 3:1–5), you will no doubt look back at yourself and say with John Newton, "Amazing grace that saved a wretch like me." You will agree that the word "wretch" is well-chosen to describe how vile you were, because you will see yourself in truth—as a selfish, sin-loving contemptible person who advocated the murder of children in the womb. You will enter with your evil heart smiling, and come out grief-stricken and horrified at what you see.

May that day come quickly, not only for the sake of your own salvation, but for the sake of the thousands who will legally die today at the end of a sharp scalpel. May it come quickly so that your vote won't be a vote that elevates prosperity above morality, as did the Germans vote not so long ago. Please, never ever vote for a man or a woman who believes that it is a right to kill the unborn.

As we have seen earlier, there are a number of

theories as the why Hitler so hated the Jews, but his motive may have been more than pure hatred-- because there is one incentive that isn't often mentioned. Adolf Hitler had a huge inducement to kill Jews: their blood financed his war-machine. He seized the assets of Jewish families, and each family he murdered added up to multiple billions of dollars. According to the experts, he financed a massive 30 percent of the German war effort by killing Jews and stealing their wealth." Jewish murder was a lucrative and lawful business in Germany--from the taking of their homes, their paintings, their savings, the gold in their teeth, to their hair—all of it added up to money in the bank for Hitler.

American abortion has the same big incentive. If you don't believe that it's a huge money-making scheme, check out your local provider's current prices. They will kill your baby for just $765 for up to a 16-week-old child, but the price increases if the baby is over 19 weeks. You will be shelling out three times the amount, and paying a whopping $2,165 (see http://www.fpamg.net/fees for current prices). That's pretty good income for a few minutes of ripping off the arms, the legs, and head of a baby onto a table; checking the body parts to make sure they're all out, and then putting them in the trash. It's just

10-15 minutes work for a skilled physician. And it's all legal, just like the Holocaust.

So it's no real mystery as to what drove Hitler to kill six million Jews, as it's no mystery as to why those who favor abortion are so zealous to make sure women have the choice when it comes to terminating their pregnancy. The love of money is still the root of all evil.

· Endnotes ·

CHAPTER 1

1. Ian Kershaw, Hitler: A Biography (New York: W. W. Norton & Co., 1998, 2008, 2008), 5–6.
2. Adolf Hitler, Mein Kampf, James Murphy translation (1939; repr., Boring, OR: CPA Book Publisher, 1942), 22.
3. Ibid., 22–23.
4. Ibid., 80.

CHAPTER 2

1. Kershaw, Hitler, 61–62.
2. Hitler, Mein Kampf, 129.
3. Kershaw, Hitler, 77–78.
4. Hitler, Mein Kampf, 276.
5. Kershaw, Hitler, 105.
6. Ibid., 111.

CHAPTER 3

1. William L. Shirer, The Rise and Fall of the Third Reich: A History of Nazi Germany, 1st Touchstone ed. (New York: Simon & Schuster, 1990), 119.
2. Kershaw, Hitler, 171.
3. Ibid., 181.
4. Ibid., 182.
5. Ibid., 192.
6. "The Rise of Adolf Hitler: Germans Elect Nazis," The History Place, http://www.historyplace.com/worldwar2/riseofhitler/elect.htm.
7. Kershaw, Hitler, 212.
8. Ibid., 210.
9. Ibid., 213.
10. Ibid., 234.
11. Ibid., 238.
12. Ibid., 255.
13. Shirer, The Rise and Fall of the Third Reich, 5.

14. Kershaw, Hitler, 256.
15. Shirer, The Rise and Fall of the Third Reich, 194.
16. Hitler, Mein Kampf, 86.
17. Göetz Aly, in Jody K. Biehl, "New Holocaust Book, New Theory: How Germans Fell for the 'Feel-Good' Fuehrer," March 22, 2005, Spiegel Online, http://www.spiegel.de/international/0,1518,347726,00.html.
18. Biehl, "New Holocaust Book, New Theory."

CHAPTER 4

1. Joseph Goebbels, The Goebbels Diaries, 1942–1943 (n.p.: Greenwood Press, 1970), 359.
2. Norman Rich, of Hitler's War Aims: Ideology, the Nazi State, and the Course of Expansion (New York: W. W. Norton, 1973), xiii.
3. Hitler, Mein Kampf, 156.
4. Adolf Hitler, Mein Kampf, transl. James Murphy (New York: Hurst and Blackett, 1982), vol. 2, chapt. 2, http://gutenberg. net.au/ebooks 02/0200601.txt.
5. David Welch, Hitler (London, UCL Press, 1998), 37.
6. Eduard Bloch, "My Patient, Hitler: A Memoir of Hitler's Jewish Physician, printed in Journal of Historical Review 14, no. 3 (May–June 1994): 27–35, available at http://www.ihr.org/jhr/mypatienthitler.html.
7. Kitty Werthmann, "Freedoms Can Disappear in a Hurry If We Aren't Careful, Eagle Forum, http://www.eagleforum.org/misc/states/articles/2003/werthmann-3-11-03.shtml.
8. Neville Chamberlain, in a speech given on September 30, 1938, available at http://eudocs.lib.byu.edu/index.php/Neville_Chamberlain%27s_%22Peace_For_Our_Time%22_speech.
9. "Suicides: Nazis go down to defeat in a wave of selbstmord," Life magazine, May 14, 1945. Viewable at http://books.google.com/books?id=CUoEAAAAMBAJ&lpg=PP1&pg=PA32#v=onepage&q&f=false.
10. "Joseph Goebbels: 'The Poison Dwarf,'" Holocaust Education & Archive Research Team, http://www.holocaustresearchproject.org/holoprelude/goebbels.html.
11. Toby Thacker, Joseph Goebbels: Life and Death (London: Palgrave, 2009), 301.
12. Nazi Conspiracy and Aggression, vol. 6 (Washington, DC: Government Printing Office, 1946–1948), 259–60.

13. "Adolf Hitler, final political testament (April 29, 1945)," Learntoquestion.com: Resources Database, posted September 29, 2005, http://www.learntoquestion.com/resources/database/archives/000752.html.

CHAPTER 5

1. Adolf Hitler, "Free State or Slavery" (speech given in Munich, July 28, 1922), http://www.hitler.org/speeches/07-28-22.html.
2. John Toland, Adolf Hitler (London: Book Club Associates, 1977), 116.
3. Hitler, Mein Kampf (CPA repr.), 39.
4. Ibid.
5. Ibid., 44–45.
6. Hitler, Mein Kampf (Hurst and Blackett), http://gutenberg.net.au/ebooks02/0200601.txt.
7. See "The International Jew by Henry Ford," http://www.reformation.org/ford-international-jew.html.
8. See "Henry Ford," http://www.holocaust-history.org/questions/ford-henry.shtml. For more on Henry Ford's anti-Semitism, see Neil Baldwin, Henry Ford and the Jews: The Mass Production of Hate (New York: Public Affairs, 2002).
9. Adolf Hitler, quoted in Michael Dobbs, "Ford and GM Scrutinized for Alleged Nazi Collaboration," Washington Post, November 30, 1998, A01, http://www.washingtonpost.com/wp-srv/national/daily/nov98/nazicars30.htm.
10. Shirer, The Rise and Fall of the Third Reich, 101.
11. Richard Wagner, Judaism in Music, and Other Essays, William Ashton Ellis, trans. (University of Nebraska Press, 1995), page numbers unknown.
12. Richard Wagner Quotes, http://www.quotesby.net/Richard-Wagner.
13. Richard Wagner, Judaism in Music, William Ashton Ellis, trans., Wagner Library ed. 1.1 (1850), http://users.belgacom.net/wagner-library/prose/wagjuda.htm.
14. Ibid.
15. Ibid.
16. Ronald Taylor, in Joachim Köhler, Wagner's Hitler: The Prophet and His Disciple (Cambridge, UK: Polity, 2001), introduction.
17. Shirer, The Rise and Fall of the Third Reich, 108.
18. R. Stackelberg and S. A. Winkle, eds., The Nazi Germany Sourcebook: An Anthology of Texts (n.p., Routeledge, 2002), 84–85.
19. Charles Darwin, quoted in The World's Most Famous Court Trial

by John Thomas Scopes (Clark, NJ: The Lawbook Exchange, Ltd., 2008), 335, http://books.google.com/books?id=rndb5m5xNk0C& pg=PA335&lpg=PA335&dq#v=onepage&q&f=false.

20. Hitler, Mein Kampf (CPA repr.), 146.
21. Ibid., 161.
22. Ibid., 161–62.
23. Ibid., 164.
24. Ibid., 163.
25. Rudolf Hess, in a meeting in 1934.
26. Henry Ford, in "The Jew in Character," Dearborn Independent, May 22, 1920, http://www.jrbooksonline.com/Intl_Jew_full_version/ij01.htm.
27. Kershaw, Hitler, 449.
28. Ibid., 469.
29. Michael Berenbaum, The World Must Know: The History of the Holocaust as Told in the United States Holocaust Memorial Museum (Boston: Little, Brown,1993), 93.
30. Franciszek Piper. "Gas Chambers and Crematoria," in Anatomy of the Auschwitz Death Camp edited by Michael Berenbaum and Yisrael Gutman (Bloomington: Indiana University Press and the United States Holocaust Museum, 1994), 173.
31. Ibid., 163, 173.
32. Berenbaum, The World Must Know, 194–95.

CHAPTER 6

1. Hitler, Mein Kampf (CPA repr.), 125.
2. See "Top Nazi Rudolf Hess Exhumed from 'Pilgrimage' Grave," July 21, 2011, Free Republic, http://www.freerepublic.com/focus/f-news/2751712/posts.
3. Norman H. Baynes, ed., The Speeches of Adolf Hitler, April 1922–August 1939, vol. 1 (London: Oxford University Press, 1942), 19–20. Adolf Hitler in a speech on April 12, 1922.
4. "Campaign against 'Godless Movement,'" Associated Press, February 23, 1933, article reprinted at http://www.infidels.org/library/historical/unknown/hitler.html.
5. Joe Sharkey, "Word for Word/The Case against the Nazis; How Hitler's Forces Planned to Destroy German Christianity," January 13, 2002, Correction Appended, http://www.nytimes.com/2002/01/13/weekinreview/word-for-word-case-against-nazis-hitler-s-forces-planned-destroy-german.html?pagewanted=all.

6. See Shirer, The Rise and Fall the Third Reich.

7. Ibid., 237.

8. Baynes, ed., The Speeches of Adolf Hitler, vol. 1, 386.

9. Alan Bullock, Hitler: A Study in Tyranny (New York: Harper Perennial, 1991).

10. See Uwe Siemon-Netto, "Analysis: Nazis vs. Christians," January 14, 2002, http://www.upi.com/Odd_News/2002/01/14/Analysis-Nazis-vs-Christians/UPI-55711011059133/

11. "The Nazi Master Plan: The Persecution of the Christian Churches," Rutgers Journal of Law and Religion, posted winter 2001, http://org.law.rutgers.edu/publications/law-religion/nurinst1.shtml.

12. Jonathan Steinberg, All or Nothing: The Axis and the Holocaust, 1941–1943. (London: Routledge Press, 2002), 243.

13. Albert Speer, Inside the Third Reich, transs. by Richard Winston, Clara Winston, and Eugene Davidson (New York: Macmillan, 1971), 143.

14. Konrad Heiden, A History of National Socialism (New York: A.A. Knopf, 1935), 100.

15. Shirer, The Rise and Fall the Third Reich, 240.

16. Ibid.

17. Herman Rauschning, "Preface," The Ten Commandments: Ten Short Novels of Hitler's War against the Moral Code, ed. Armin L. Robinson (New York: Simon and Schuster, 1943), xiii.

18. John Lennon, quoted in Maureen Cleave, "The John Lennon I Knew," Telegraph (UK), October 5, 2005. http://www.telegraph.co.uk/culture/music/rockandjazzmusic/3646983/The-John-Lennon-I-knew.html.

19. Albert Einstein, interviewed by George Sylvester Viereck, What Life Means to Einstein: An Interview," Saturday Evening Post, October 26, 1929, 17.

20. John Toland, Adolf Hitler (New York: Anchor Books, Doubleday, 1976), 143.

21. J. S. Conway, The Nazi Persecution of the Churches 1933–1945 (n.p.: Regent College Publishing, 1997), page number not known.

22. Jean-Denis G.G. Lepage, Hitler Youth, 1922–1945: An Illustrated History (Jefferson: McFarland & Company, 2009), 87.

23. "Hitler Becomes Führer," The History Place, http://www.history-place.com/worldwar2/holocaust/h-becomes.htm.

24. Rolf Tell, Sound and Führer (Hesperides Press, 2006). Rudolf Hess was addressing political leaders in Munich April, 21 1938.

25. Simon Berthon and Joanna Potts, Warlords: An Extraordinary Re-

creation of World War II through the Eyes and Minds of Hitler, Roosevelt, Churchill and Stalin (New York: Da Capo, 2007), 141.

26. "Fighters for the Eternal Reich," Das Reich, April 8, 1945.

27. Richard Steigman-Gall, The Holy Reich: Nazi Conceptions of Christianity, 1919–1945 (Cambridge University Press, 2003). Page number unknown.

28. Ibid.

29. Ibid.

30. Walter C. Langer and Dr. S. D. Stein, "A Psychological Profile of Adolph Hitler," (Washington: The United States Office of Strategic Services (USOSS), 1943). http://www.nizkor.org/hweb/people/h/hitler-adolf/oss-papers/ text/oss-profile-01.html.

CHAPTER 7

1. Shirer, The Rise and Fall of the Third Reich, 349.

2. "On This Day 1950–2005," BBC News online, July 20, http://news.bbc.co.uk/onthisday/hi/dates/stories/july/20/newsid_3505000/3505014.stm.

3. "Global Hunger," Bread for the World website, http://www.bread.org/hunger/global/.

4. Miranda Hitti, "Car Crashes Kill 40,000 in U.S. Every Year," FoxNews.com: Health, February 3, 2005, http://www.foxnews.com/story/0,2933,146212,00.html.

5. These quotes are among several comments received by a United States Senate judiciary subcommittee in 1981, from a collection of medical experts testifying in relation to life's beginning. For more expert testimony received by this subcommittee, along with other medical testimony concerning abortion, see "The Case against Abortion: Medical Testimony," http://www.abort73.com/abortion/medical_testimony/.

6. Ibid.